Simply . . . Gluten-free
Desserts

150 Delicious Recipes for Cupcakes,
Cookies, Pies, and More Old
and New Favorites

๑๑๑๑๑๑

Simply . . . Gluten-free
Desserts

Carol Kicinski

THOMAS DUNNE BOOKS
St. Martin's Press
New York

THOMAS DUNNE BOOKS.
An imprint of St. Martin's Press.

SIMPLY . . . GLUTEN-FREE DESSERTS. Copyright © 2011 by Carol Kicinski.
Foreword copyright © by Vikki Petersen. All rights reserved. Printed in
the United States of America. For information, address St. Martin's Press,
175 Fifth Avenue, New York, N.Y. 10010.

www.thomasdunnebooks.com

www.stmartins.com

Design by Kathryn Parise

ISBN 978-0-312-64347-8

First Edition: April 2011

10 9 8 7 6 5 4 3 2 1

For my husband, Thom,
and sons, Colin and Dustin,
who make mine a life worth celebrating

Contents

Heartfelt Thanks

If one is lucky, every once in a great while a person will enter one's life who alters the course of that life for the better and makes something magical happen. Such was the case when I met publicist Laurie Jessup. Laurie saw in my blog something she believed in and asked an editor at Thomas Dunne Books, Peter Joseph, to take a look. At a time when the safe bet would be to publish a cookbook from a celebrity chef, Peter took a risk on me and shared my vision for a mainstream book on gluten-free baking. Without the confidence and support of Laurie and Peter this book would not exist. Laurie and Peter would never have known about me if my good friend Jan Meekoms had not introduced Laurie to my blog Simply Gluten-free, www.simplygluten-free .com, an introduction for which I am immensely grateful.

I consider myself extremely fortunate to have not one but two friends who were willing to drop everything, fly three thousand miles, and give up a week or two of their lives for no other reason than because I asked. In what I now think of as photography boot camp, good friend and photographer extraordinaire Derek Geer taught me what all the wheels, gizmos, and thingamabobs on my camera were and how to use them, tutored me on the use of Photoshop, and lived on nothing but dessert for days on end. No matter how late at night I called him, he never failed to pick up the phone and talk me through a technical issue with incredible patience and care. It is because of Derek that I was able to shoot all the photos in this book.

When I finally came up with a gluten-free flour blend that met all my requirements it was important to get an expert opinion. Cordon Bleu–trained chef and dear friend Darrell Malick tested my flour blend in recipe after recipe, putting it through vigorous tests to ensure it would function as well, if not better, than all-purpose wheat flour. Darrell explained to me the chemistry of why things I did instinctively in the kitchen worked and helped me find a better way if they didn't. He helped me perfect basic recipes, such as my pie crust, tried (unsuccessfully) to teach me how to use the mathematical constant *pi* to figure how to increase or decrease the size of a pie crust, and refrained (only slightly more successfully) from grimacing at my unprofessional knife skills.

Doctors Vikki and Rick Petersen were responsible for originally diagnosing me with gluten intolerance and taught me how to take greater responsibility for my own health. As a result of their care not only has my health improved but my life's direction was changed for the better. They became my great friends and have even taken time out of their insanely busy schedules to test my sweet rice flour blend and many of these recipes.

My blog readers are a constant source of inspiration and encouragement. They comprise a virtual neighborhood of like-minded people, determined to live and eat well despite the lack of gluten in our lives.

When it came time for recipe testing I turned to where it all started for me, the Internet. I asked for help and my blog readers and Twitter pals responded. Shari Shacchi (www.tickledred.com), Jennifer Miller Kelly (www.cinnamon quill.com), Kim Maes (www.cookitallergyfree.com), Deanna Schneider (www .themommybowl.com), Susan M. Gudenkauf (www.twitter.com/susangude), Autumn Giles (www.asbadasitlooks.wordpress.com), Barb Lance (www.wix.com/ pchefbarb), Alessio Fangano (www.recipetaster.blogspot.com), Carrie Forbes (www.gingerlemongirl.com), Kristin Crump (www.glutenfreecrumpette.blogspot .com), and Sara La Fountain answered my plea for help, cooked and baked numerous recipes, offered their critiques and praise, and best of all, enriched my world by becoming my friends.

Without my girlfriends my life would lack the support system on which I so rely. My beautiful friends Angie Moore, Jude Barnes, and Randee Johnston lent me not only their encouragement and support but china, teacups, and fabrics, which added color and texture to the photos and made up for my love of white dishes. They offered help and advice, tested recipes, and dragged me off to the movies when I needed to get out of the kitchen. If these gals were not in my world it would be a little less bright, a little less funny, and a lot less rich.

Shannon Byrnes and Rachael Bradham rolled up their sleeves and washed my dishes on more occasions that I can recall. They offered opinions and helped with photo styling, ironed napkins, taste-tested countless recipes, and made emergency grocery-store runs.

It is fortuitous that I am blessed with two terrific sisters. Katherine O'Neal, twelve-time published novelist, offered excellent big sisterly advice on the ins and outs of writing a book, taught me how to manage the workload, and encouraged me every step of the way. Karen O'Neal has been an advocate of this endeavor from the beginning, offering dessert suggestions, testing recipes, and cheering me on.

My grandchildren, Julian and Milla Kicinski, were my secret co-conspirators in putting together the proposal for this book. They eagerly offered to taste-test recipes, helped me set up photo shoots, and cheered when the book deal was confirmed. And, probably hardest of all, they kept my secret until I was willing to tell the world.

My mother's love for entertaining and her dramatic flair for presentation planted the seeds of culinary creativity in my imagination at a very young age.

I honestly do not know where I would be without the men in my life. My father taught me that it was possible to accomplish anything, and he raised my sisters and me with love, care, and an amazing amount of tolerance. My sons, Colin and Dustin, are my greatest source of joy; I am so proud of the men they have become. My husband, Thom, has been a constant in my life from the moment I met him at the tender age of seventeen. He has supported and encouraged me in every way possible. He has given me a life filled with love and adventure. Thom is, quite simply, my everything.

To these people I offer my sincere and heartfelt thanks.

Foreword

Diagnosing gluten sensitivity in all its forms and treating the secondary effects associated with it comprises a good part of what I do. While our clinic sees patients presenting with all types of health problems, realizing the pervasiveness of gluten sensitivity as a root cause beneath so many conditions prompted us to write our first book, *The Gluten Effect*, in 2009.

When you are diagnosed with celiac disease or gluten sensitivity, be it from a blood test, biopsy, or self-diagnosis, there is a distinct period of confusion. Foods you have always reached for are suddenly forbidden. What used to seemingly be "comfort" food is suddenly more like "rat poison."

I grew up in a household where my mother loved to cook and I was well trained as a sous chef. But as a busy clinician with three small children, for many years I left the cooking to others. When my children got to a certain age, they informed me that they were tired of having nannies cook for them, they wanted their mother. I realized that I had become a bit rusty in that department and turned to my trusted friend Carol for help. Carol was known for her amazing dinner parties where everything not only tasted delicious but looked amazing as well. I'll never forget thinking to myself that "only Carol" could make a bowl of lemons look like a work of art when I saw them in her home as a centerpiece.

With Carol's help, I not only began cooking again but I became rehabilitated as a cook. The excitement and joy of creating in the kitchen was restored and it continues to this day.

I was able to return the favor several years later when Carol came to see me professionally for some health complaints. While she wasn't overjoyed at the

diagnosis initially, discovering her gluten sensitivity definitely created positive effects for her.

Like all of us who undergo a major dietary change, Carol was initially challenged in the kitchen. But in short order she not only embraced the gluten-free lifestyle but has become very well known because of it. Talk about turning lemons into lemonade!

Carol's blog, Simply Gluten-free, is a sheer delight. Not only are the recipes amazing but I'll tell you a little secret; I read the blog when I want a little stress relief. As you will see in this book, Carol is not only a wonderful gluten-free chef, she's very funny! It's a real talent to make people laugh out loud from your written word and Carol has that ability. Her blog recipes run the gamut from the simple healthy salad to the more extravagant dinner party, and she holds your hand throughout the entire process, ensuring your successful outcome.

You're in for a real treat with *Simply . . . Gluten-free Desserts*. There is a tremendous breadth of variety; something to try for every occasion, including just a treat for yourself after a long day.

Enjoy!

To your good health,

DR. VIKKI PETERSEN, DC, CCN
Author of *The Gluten Effect*
Cofounder of HealthNOW Medical Center
www.glutendoctors.blogspot.com

Introduction

ᔕᔕᔕᔕᔕᔕᔕᔕᔕ

I am the middle of three daughters born to an American Air Force pilot and an English artist. Growing up I traveled extensively with my family. My mother always encouraged us to try new things and to be fearless in eating, and I learned early on to appreciate food from a variety of cultures.

At home we ate a fairly typical diet, which included many wheat-based products. Little did we know at the time that the wheat breads and breakfast cereals I was eating were slowly eroding my small intestine and poisoning my body. By the time I was in my mid-thirties I was suffering from an average of two migraine headaches a week, was severely exhausted, and had constant digestive problems.

The only "cure" for gluten intolerance is to adopt a gluten-free diet. When I discovered I was gluten intolerant I was taken aback. Half of my family can tolerate gluten and half not. I needed to find a way to prepare meals we would all enjoy, and I needed to figure out how to do so without the gluten-filled ingredients so familiar to me.

When I looked to gluten-free cookbooks for inspiration I was disheartened. They lacked the beautiful, glossy photographs that I so enjoy. The books were, for the most part, printed on inexpensive paper, read like textbooks, and often contained ingredients not commonly found in the average grocery store. They seemed to be written for the "sick person" or "allergy person," relegated to the alternative diet category. They did not seem to be written for people like me, people who love great food.

So I turned to food itself for inspiration. It was then that I decided to look at the world of food not in terms of what I can't eat but what I can eat. I discovered

a whole beautiful, abundant world of gluten-free food. I started to create and cook dishes that would not only keep me from being ill but were delicious and aestheticly pleasing as well. I cooked food that was not just fit for people with a food intolerance but also fit for people who truly love to eat.

My philosophy is simple: find great food that is naturally gluten-free. I love the challenge of discovering how to re-invent old favorites, simply and gluten-free. I have never been big on self-deprivation and denial. I choose instead to celebrate the abundance of a gluten-free lifestyle. And what would a celebration be without dessert? Whether it is the finale to an elegant dinner party, the end of a family meal, or an after-school snack with the kids, desserts and treats are the little indulgences that make life truly special. They can also be the most daunting for the gluten-free cook.

My desserts and treats are not only gluten-free but many are grain- and dairy-free as well. They can be made with readily available ingredients and require no special equipment and no more expertise than the average home cook already possesses.

I hope you enjoy this book and find in it recipes that will help you to celebrate the special moments, big or small, of your life.

Gluten-free Cooking and Baking

Making delicious gluten-free desserts without wheat flour is entirely possible. All of my recipes have been taste-tested by people who are not gluten-free to ensure they are not just "good for gluten-free" but are good, period.

My hope is that this cookbook will be a springboard for you. Many of the recipes can be mixed and matched, allowing you to come up with your own personal creations. Don't be afraid to try new things. Cooking, after all, isn't brain surgery; it needn't be serious or arduous. Have fun. Experiment. Sometimes we learn more from our failures than our successes. The best part of learning to cook and bake gluten-free is eating the results afterward!

Ingredients

As with anything, in cooking the best results come from starting with the best ingredients. Use fruits and vegetables that are ripe and in season, keep your flours and nuts fresh by storing them in the freezer and, if you can afford it, buy organic butter and eggs. Here is a list of ingredients I use over and over again in my recipes.

Agave Nectar. Previously available only in health food stores, agave nectar is now widely available. I live in a small town and can find it in the regular grocery store. It has a much lower glycemic index than sugar. The light agave is closest to the flavor of granulated sugar and the amber has a richer, almost caramel flavor that pairs well with coffee and chocolate.

Almond Flour. For grain-free desserts almond flour is a terrific alternative.

I use only finely ground, blanched almond flour. It is available in health food stores, on the Internet, and some grocery stores.

Baking Powder. A leavening agent that helps cakes and breads rise, I use aluminum-free, double-acting baking powder.

Baking Soda. For recipes that contain acid such as citrus juice or buttermilk, baking soda helps them rise. I use Arm & Hammer baking soda.

Butter. I only use unsalted butter. I like salt as much (if not more) than the next guy but I like to control the amount of salt that goes into my food. If you only have salted butter, make sure to decrease the amount of salt in the recipe. People who can't tolerate dairy can usually use organic butter as it is virtually free of the milk proteins that are normally problematic. However, I am not a doctor so please get expert advice on this if dairy is an issue. Good-quality, dairy-free butter substitutes such as Earth Balance can easily be substituted for butter in my recipes.

Buttermilk. Some of my recipes call for buttermilk. The acid in the buttermilk makes for a tender final product. If you don't have buttermilk on hand, you can make your own substitute by adding 1 tablespoon of freshly squeezed lemon juice or white vinegar to every cup of milk or dairy-free milk. Stir and let sit for 5 minutes before using.

Chocolate. Many chocolate chips (especially store brands) contain vegetable oil fillers. I prefer to use premium chocolate and chocolate chips. Ghirardelli is a trusted brand that is available in most grocery stores. Bittersweet or dark chocolate should be at least 60 percent cacao. Look for dairy-free chocolate if you can't tolerate dairy.

Citrus Juice and Zest. Please, please, please use freshly squeezed citrus juice and freshly grated citrus zest. The imitation stuff just doesn't taste the same and as always, fresh is best.

Coconut Milk. This is my favorite dairy substitute for baking and making desserts. As coconut milk will separate in the can (the fat rising to the top) it is very important to shake the can well before using. When using only part of a

can of coconut milk in a recipe I always pour it from the can into a clear jar with a lid. It stores well in the refrigerator, and I can see that the coconut milk and fat are properly combined.

Cornmeal. Ground from corn, cornmeal comes in white and yellow varieties and various grinds. I use it to add a rustic texture to cakes and muffins.

Cream. Unless stated otherwise, I use heavy whipping cream in all recipes that call for cream. Heavy cream has a higher fat content than whipping cream and will hold up longer allowing you to prepare your desserts ahead of time without losing volume or quality.

Dairy. About half the people who are gluten intolerant can't tolerate dairy, either. Many recipes in this book are specifically dairy-free but for those that are not you can usually substitute nondairy milk. I prefer to use coconut milk in baking and cooking.

Eggs. I always bake with large eggs, and whenever possible I prefer to use organic.

Espresso Powder. I use instant espresso powder for baking to make coffee-flavored dishes and to intensify the taste of chocolate. Instant espresso powder is available in most grocery stores but if you can't find it just use instant coffee granules. Decaf is fine.

Extracts. Use only pure vanilla or almond extracts, not imitation. Imitation extracts are not only inferior in taste but can contain gluten.

Flours. There are a variety of gluten-free flours available at health food stores and on the Internet. A partial list includes white rice flour, brown rice flour, sweet rice (or glutinous) flour, amaranth flour, buckwheat flour, chestnut flour, coconut flour, cornmeal, millet flour, quinoa flour, sorghum flour, tapioca flour, and teff flour. No one flour can be successfully substituted for wheat flour. See more on this in the section on Sweet Rice Flour Blend (page 14).

Liqueurs. Most liqueurs are gluten-free due to the distillation process. If you are not sure about a specific product, check the manufacturer's Web site for allergen information.

Nonstick Cooking Spray. Look for sprays that contain *only* oil. Some brands add flour, which is definitely *not* gluten-free.

Oats. For a long time oats were forbidden on a gluten-free diet. This was not because the oats themselves contain gluten but because of the growing and milling practices, which allowed the oats to be contaminated with gluten. Look for certified gluten-free oats.

Oil. As a rule I prefer grapeseed oil in baking. It can withstand high temperatures, is loaded with antioxidants, and has a neutral taste. Any neutral-tasting oil can be substituted.

Salt. My recipes call for kosher or fine sea salt. If you use table salt decrease the amount of salt called for by half.

Spices. Use only fresh, good-quality spices. It is a good idea to go through your spice cabinet every six months and purge the old and replace with the new. If possible buy whole spices and grind or grate as needed.

Starches. Used for thickening sauces and adding bulk and texture to baked goods, starches are an important element in gluten-free cooking. For thickening puddings, sauces, and custards my recipes call for cornstarch as it is readily available. For people with a sensitivity to corn, arrowroot can be substituted for cornstarch using a 2:3 ratio; 2 teaspoons of arrowroot equals 1 tablespoon of cornstarch. Arrowroot has a tendency to become slimy when mixed with milk products. Tapioca is a neutral-flavored starch that is excellent when made into pudding and my choice of thickener for fruit pies. It is important to use instant (minute) tapioca or tapioca starch when baking pies.

Sugar. I stock pure cane granulated, brown, and confectioners' sugar. Each has its own unique qualities and purposes.

Xanthan Gum. Without gluten, flour lacks elasticity and baked goods will not rise properly or hold together when baked. For people with corn allergies guar gum can be substituted using a 1:1 ratio. Xanthan and guar gums may seem to be expensive ingredients but a little goes a long way, and they last almost indefinitely stored in an airtight container in the freezer. Guar gum is much

less expensive than xanthan gum. Both can be found at health food stores and on the Internet.

Equipment

One needn't acquire every kitchen gadget or piece of equipment to produce good food. Having some basics, however, makes life so much easier. Here is a list of what I consider the essentials.

Electric Mixer. I used to think cookbook authors who started a recipe with "In an electric mixer fitted with the paddle attachment..." were pretentious. This was before my husband bought me a KitchenAid stand mixer. When I state using a paddle or whisk attachment realize that this is the preferred way, not the only way. For years and years I got along just fine with nothing but an electric hand mixer. In an ideal world one would possess both a stand and hand mixer.

Food Processor. Cooking is certainly possible without a food processor, but once one has gotten used to the ease and quickness of food prep using one, it's hard to go back. I have three food processors of different sizes, which may be a tad excessive, however when one has only a half cup of nuts to chop, it is a joy not to have to drag out the heavy machinery when my mini food processor works just great.

Blender. Often the food processor can be substituted for a blender, but there are times when the blender is more efficient and less messy. Mine has only one speed, high, and I have never found myself thinking "Gee, I wish it had nine more speeds."

Ice Cream Maker. Nothing can compare to homemade ice cream. You control the quality and freshness of the ingredients and can create any flavor your heart desires. This is especially essential if dairy is an issue for you. I prefer the electric kind where you freeze the bowl; much simpler and less messy than the old-fashioned, hand-crank variety.

Silicone Baking Mats. Years ago these nonstick miracle baking mats were expensive and could only be found in gourmet kitchen stores, but now they are readily available. I have owned the same pair for more than twelve years and when I think of the amount of parchment paper I would have used instead, they would still have been a bargain at twice the price. No matter how nonstick your baking pans claim to be, nothing can compare to these baking mats, and they are much easier to clean than a baking sheet.

Ice Cream Scoops. Not just for ice cream, these spring-action scoops are great for measuring out batter cookies and cupcakes. Not only is the batter easier to scoop but the portions will be the same, ensuring even baking. I have an assortment of sizes.

Knives. The first investment any cook should make is in a set of good, sharp knives. With proper care, good-quality knives can last a lifetime.

Pots and Pans. Another essential investment for every kitchen is a set of good-quality, heavy-duty pots, pans, and skillets. Thin saucepans can't stand up to really high temperatures for tasks such as making caramel. I also believe every cook should have a well-seasoned, cast-iron skillet.

Baking Pans. It is a good idea to have an array of baking pans, baking sheets, pie plates, muffin pans, and such. I prefer heavy-duty pans as they ensure proper baking, even browning, and don't warp in the oven. I have muffin pans in three sizes: mini, standard, and large. I also can't live without a spring-form pan. With cake pans it is always a good idea to have a pair in a matching size; this way you can bake layer cakes in one go. Flat baking sheets are best for cookies, and rimmed baking sheets are useful for making cookie bars.

Mixing Bowls. I have a variety of sizes of mixing bowls in both glass and metal. Glass can go in the microwave, and metal can be put on top of a pan of simmering water for gentle cooking or melting, eliminating the need for a double boiler. Plastic bowls get scratched and warp over time.

Strainer. A strainer is a great multitask piece of equipment that can be used for draining off liquids, removing seeds from berry sauces, and sifting and dusting cocoa powder or confectioners' sugar on top of finished desserts. A tiny strainer is handy when you need to dust cocoa or confectioners' sugar onto something small like a muffin or cupcake.

Wire Cooling Racks. Wire racks allow the air to circulate when cooling baked goods; important in stopping residual cooking.

Spatulas. I am in love with silicone spatulas and have replaced all my old rubber variety spatulas with them. They come in an array of shapes and sizes, are flexible enough to fold egg whites or whipped cream, and will not melt when used in a pan of hot liquid. I also have flexible and sturdy metal spatulas for removing cookies from baking sheets and flipping crepes and what not. It is a good idea to have offset spatulas as well. They make the job of frosting cakes and cupcakes so much easier. I have two sizes, one small one for cupcakes and cookies and one large one for cakes.

Measuring Cups and Spoons. Liquid and dry ingredients are measured differently and for that reason it is a must to have dry and liquid measuring cups. I prefer to have a liquid measuring cup that is heatproof so I can put it in the microwave or pour hot liquid into it without the fear of melting. Dry measuring cups and measuring spoons should be constructed so it is easy to scoop the ingredients into them and level off the excess.

Whisks. It is a good idea to have an assortment of whisks on hand for mixing; in most cases they are more effective than using a spoon. If I have just a little bit of cream to whip, I will use a whisk instead of dragging out the heavy artillery.

Pastry Brush. Use for brushing off excess flour, topping scones with cream, or tidying up the final look of cookies. Look for well-made, good quality brushes with bristles that won't come off on your food. They now make silicone pastry brushes that also work very well.

Microplane Grater. The easiest way to grate ingredients such as chocolate, nutmeg, or cinnamon is with a Microplane grater. It also makes zesting fresh citrus an easy chore.

Oven Thermometer. Oven temperatures vary, often widely. I have two ovens; one runs about 25 degrees cool and the other almost 75 degrees hot. For this reason I suggest buying an oven thermometer; inexpensive ones can be found in almost any hardware or grocery store.

Kitchen Timer. When baked goods are in the oven I don't necessarily want to stay in the kitchen waiting for them. I like a timer I can carry with me so I don't risk burning my desserts.

Parchment Paper. While I do rely on my silicone baking mats I still stock parchment paper for lining cake pans, cooling nut pralines, and such. It does not burn in the oven and, unlike wax paper, will not leave wax on your baked goods.

Plastic Food Storage Bags. As well as using them for storing food, I fill the bags with frosting or cream, snip off the end, and use as a piping bag. They are disposable, work well, and are less messy than traditional pastry bags.

Paper Muffin Liners. Eliminating the need to grease and flour your muffin pans, paper liners also make for easy cleanup when baking muffins and cupcakes. They come in a variety of colors and styles, including silicone muffin liners, which can be washed and reused.

Cooking and Baking Tips

With a few basic tips you can be baking gluten-free like a pro. In this book I include the tips specific for each recipe to ensure that you get a good result. Here are some general tips you may also find useful.

Room Temperature Ingredients. When baking, often the recipe will call for room-temperature ingredients. Having all the ingredients at room temperature will ensure better blending of the batter and a more even baking time. Take the ingredients out of the refrigerator 20 to 30 minutes before starting the recipe. When a recipe calls for separated eggs at room temperature, it is easier to separate the whites from the yolks when the eggs are cold. Separate them first and then let them come to room temperature. Butter and cream cheese must be at room temperature before creaming to ensure that the air is whipped in properly.

Measuring. For dry ingredients scoop the ingredients into the measuring cup and scrape off the excess with a flat edge such as the back of a knife. The same holds true for spices; scoop then scrape. Dry ingredients should never be measured in a liquid measuring cup; the amount will not be the same as in a dry measure.

Adding Eggs to Batters. Most recipes will call for adding the eggs one at a time and mixing each in thoroughly before adding the next one. This is the typical method when the batter starts with creaming the butter and sugar. The reason for this is that you have just incorporated air into the butter and if the eggs are added all at once the batter could lose volume as the air pockets you have created by creaming will collapse. The batter may also break and look curdled. If the batter breaks, it is not the end of the world and the batter is still usable.

Properly Beaten Egg Whites. As you beat egg whites they go through various stages. They start off a very pale yellow color, turn foamy, get white, and finally turn into stiff peaks, which are glossy and smooth. Overbeaten whites will look lumpy, drier, and dull. They start to form clumps. Overbeaten egg whites are more likely to collapse in the oven. If you must err, err on the side of slightly underbeaten whites rather than overbeaten. The only exception would be if the recipe states to beat the whites until they are dry. The reason for this would usually be that whatever they are mixed with has a high liquid content. When adding sugar to egg whites, beat the whites until they get foamy and then gradually add the sugar. This will help to better incorporate the sugar into the whites. Always use a clean mixing bowl and clean beater for beating egg whites as any fat or oil will impede their forming stiff peaks.

Checking for Doneness. As I mentioned earlier, oven temperatures vary. It is always a good idea to check your baked goods for doneness a few minutes prior to the end of the stated baking time. In this book, I try to tell you what the recipe should look, feel, or smell like when done so you can rely on your instincts rather than baking times.

Sunken Cakes. Some gluten-free cakes will naturally sink in the middle as they cool. This would usually be the case with flourless cakes. For cakes that contain flour the reason for this could be either that the cake is not done in the middle or too much leavening was used. If the cake is baking too quickly at the edges and remains uncooked in the center, you need to turn your oven temperature down and possibly extend the baking time. If the cake rises and sinks because of too much leavening, use less. As a rule of thumb, 1 to 1¼ teaspoons of baking powder per cup of flour is ideal. In recipes calling for baking soda, ¼ to ½ teaspoon is usually sufficient for each cup of flour. Baking soda is only used when the ingredients include an acid such as citrus juice, buttermilk, sour cream, or yogurt.

Proper Mixing. While I love to mix batter with my stand mixer I always give a final mix with a spatula to ensure all the ingredients are properly mixed. There is just no way for the beaters of a mixer to do a thorough job. This seems to be especially important with gluten-free baking. Overmixing can cause heavy cakes. While some think that this is from stimulating the gluten (which would make this a needless worry in gluten-free baking), actually what happens is overmixing destroys the tiny air bubbles you have incorporated into the batter, thus causing a heavy cake.

Adding Flour in Batches. Most cake and cupcake recipes will ask you to add the flour in either two or three stages, alternating with whatever liquid is going into the batter. This ensures proper mixing without overworking the batter.

Folding in Ingredients. Folding in is a way to combine ingredients without knocking out the air; this is typically used when working with beaten egg whites or cream. A rubber or silicone spatula is the best tool for the job. To properly fold in ingredients take some of the lighter mixture (such as beaten egg whites or cream) and mix it with the heavier mixture (such as chocolate or beaten egg yolks), then take the rest of the lighter ingredients and add it to that mixture (lighter on top of heavier). Using the spatula, reach down to the bottom of the mixing bowl and lift some of the heavier ingredients up and onto the lighter ingredients. Turn the bowl about a quarter of a turn and repeat until the mixtures are combined. Use quick, fluid strokes and try to incorporate the ingredients with as few strokes as possible. Don't be timid! The longer it takes you to combine the ingredients, the more the air bubbles are deflated. Combine just until the mixture is no longer streaky in appearance.

Settling the Batter. Rapping a cake or muffin pan on the counter a few times will force air bubbles to the top and ensures even baking. It also helps even out the batter so it is not higher on one side than the other.

Rotating Pans During Baking. Some parts of an oven are usually hotter than others. Rotating the pans a quarter-turn halfway through the baking time ensures even baking. If pans are placed on two different racks in the oven (one higher up than the other), switch them as well.

Oven Rack Position. Unless the recipe states otherwise, place the oven rack in the middle of the oven, which is best for baking.

Whipped Cream. For the best result use heavy whipping cream. It has a higher fat content and will stay whipped longer. It is a good idea to start with a cold mixing bowl and cold beaters. Add sugar (if called for in the recipe) before beating the cream and add any extracts after the cream starts to form peaks. Do not overbeat cream or it will turn into butter. Whipped cream can be prepared ahead of time, especially if you use heavy whipping cream. A little tip is to put the whipped cream into a strainer placed over a bowl, and keep it in the refrigerator until ready to serve; any liquid that seeps out will drain off.

Stabilized Whipped Cream. Whipped cream makes a simple and delicious frosting for cakes, it can however make the cake harder to store or transport as the cream can start to melt. Stabilizing the whipped cream helps solve the problem. For every 1 cup of cream you will need 1 tablespoon cold water and ½ teaspoon unflavored gelatin. Pour the water into a small microwave-safe bowl. Sprinkle the gelatin on the water and let it set for 5 minutes. This is called "blooming the gelatin." Microwave the bloomed gelatin for 10 seconds on high power, or until it is melted but not hot. Whip the cream until it starts to stiffen up. Add the gelatin all at once and continue to whip until soft or stiff peaks form. If you are sweetening the cream, add sugar to the heavy cream before starting to whip it. Add any extract after the peaks have formed.

Saving Egg Whites and Yolks. Often a recipe will call for just the egg whites or just the yolks. Whenever just the yolks are needed, do not toss out the whites. Egg whites can be stored in a covered container in the refrigerator for several days; in fact macaroons are best made with "old" egg whites. For longer-term storage, drop the individual egg whites into the cubes of an ice cube tray. Freeze and then pop the cubes into a freezer-weight plastic storage bag. Simply thaw and use when needed. Yolks dry out after a day or two in the refrigerator. If possible, keep the yolks whole and drop into a container with water; this will prevent them drying out. Yolks can be stored, refrigerated, for up to two days.

Nondairy Whipped "Cream." A good nondairy substitute for whipped cream is whipped coconut milk. Refrigerate 3 cans of full-fat coconut milk until cold. Refrigerate a mixing bowl and beaters. Open the cans with a can opener that completely removes the top of the can. Skim the cream from the top being careful not to get any of the liquid from the bottom of the can. Whip the coconut cream with 2 tablespoons of granulated sugar until thick and stiff. Add vanilla or other extract, if desired. Store in the refrigerator until ready to use.

Sweet Rice Flour Blend

No single flour can replace wheat flour in gluten-free baking. Gluten is a sticky protein found in wheat, rye, barley, and other grains. It is what makes pizza dough stretchy, cakes rise, and baked goods hold together. Gluten-free flours need to be combined with starches and gums in order to react the same way that wheat flour does. Most gluten-free cooking and baking failures occur when the flour blend used does not contain enough starch and gum additives to make up for the lack of sticking power found in gluten. When I first went gluten-free I shied away from traditional baking because it seemed like too much trouble to combine various flours. I soon found that in reality it takes only a few short minutes to mix up a batch of gluten-free flour blend.

There are commercially produced gluten-free flour blends available at health food stores and on the Internet, and recently I have started to see some brands showing up on regular grocery store shelves. You can use those pre-packaged blends in the recipes in this book, but I find these products are usually too gritty for my tastes, something especially unappealing when it comes to desserts.

After much trial and error I finally came up with a flour blend that works perfectly in gluten-free baking. This is my preferred flour mix and can be substituted for wheat flour cup for cup. It is called Carol's Amazing All Purpose Gluten-Free Flour and is available commercially.

I also developed a recipe for a flour blend you can make at home that will give you very similar results.

You are going to love this flour mixture. Believe me when I say no one can tell the final product is gluten-free. I taste-tested this flour blend on many, many people who customarily eat wheat and quite a few who shy away from "alternative foods." The comments were unanimously very positive; people either could not tell the desserts were gluten-free or, in fact, preferred the dishes to those prepared with wheat flour.

The ingredients in this blend are white rice flour, sweet (or glutinous) rice flour, tapioca starch, potato starch, and xanthan gum.

White Rice Flour. Not all rice flours are created equally. I prefer to use superfine rice flour or Asian rice flour. Superfine white rice flour is available on

the Internet and in health food stores and Asian white rice flour is available in Asian markets, on the Internet, and in some grocery stores in the ethnic section. Superfine and Asian rice flours are much more finely milled than other rice flours. Asian cultures have been making fine delicacies with rice flour for centuries and have perfected the art of milling it. If you ever want to try a little test, rub some regular white rice flour between your thumb and forefinger and then do the same with some superfine or Asian white rice flour. You will notice the difference immediately. There is no grittiness at all with the superfine and Asian flours.

Sweet Rice Flour. Sweet rice flour is also called glutinous rice flour but don't let the name alarm you. Glutinous refers to the fact that the type of rice it is milled from is especially sticky. There is no gluten in sweet or glutinous rice flour. Again I use either superfine or Asian sweet rice flour. The addition of sweet rice flour helps with browning and makes baked goods more tender. Glutinous rice flour can also help smooth out the grittiness that comes from regular white rice flour.

Tapioca Starch. Tapioca is a gluten-free starch that can be used for thickening sauces, puddings, and pie fillings, and helps baked goods hold together. Without tapioca, baked goods would fall apart if only gluten-free flours were used. It is also sometimes called tapioca flour.

Potato Starch. Potato starch is not to be confused with potato flour; they are *not* interchangeable. Potato starch adds bulk and sticking power to gluten-free flour blends. Potato starch can be purchased in health food stores and over the Internet.

Xanthan Gum. Xanthan gum is a binding agent, which will keep your gluten-free baked goods from falling apart. It is the most expensive ingredient in this sweet rice flour blend but very little is used per batch of flour. Xanthan gum is derived from corn so if you have a sensitivity to corn substitute guar gum.

Before I make up the flour blend I empty the individual bags of flours and

starches into their own freezer-strength plastic storage bags and label them. This makes scooping and measuring easier and I store the bags in the freezer. I make up a batch of this flour blend and store it in a canister so it is always on hand when the mood to bake strikes me. You can also store it in a large plastic storage bag in the freezer.

This sweet rice flour blend is so fine it does not need to be sifted before use.

4¹⁄₂ cups white rice flour

1¹⁄₂ cups sweet (glutinous) rice flour

2 cups potato starch (not potato flour)

1 cup tapioca starch (also known as tapioca flour)

4 teaspoons xanthan gum

Measure each ingredient by scooping it into a measuring cup (or spoon), leveling it off with a straight edge, such as the back of a knife. In a large mixing bowl, whisk all ingredients together very well until they are evenly distributed. I whisk the ingredients slowly for at least a minute or two, making sure to get to the bottom of the bowl and turning the ingredients over and over.

This recipe can easily be halved, doubled, or tripled.

Cakes and Cupcakes

Flourless Chocolate Cake

• Grain-free

I have heard it said that in order to be a great cook you need to only really master ten recipes that you do well. This recipe would definitely be on my top-ten list.

The basic recipe is rich, intensely chocolaty, and great just as is but it can also be transformed in a number of ways. Cut into layers, and spread on some whipped cream and berries and it is a pretty party cake. Bake the batter in sheet pans, cut into circles, and sandwich ice cream between, and you have flourless ice cream sandwiches. Drizzle them with caramel sauce and it transforms yet again. My favorite combination is to serve with a simple raspberry sauce (thawed frozen raspberries whirled in the blender and strained) and some lightly whipped cream.

16 tablespoons (2 sticks) unsalted butter, cut into pieces plus more for preparing the pan

1½ cups semisweet chocolate chips

1¼ cups sugar

1 cup unsweetened cocoa powder, sifted

1 tablespoon instant espresso powder

Pinch kosher or fine sea salt

6 large eggs

2 teaspoons pure vanilla extract

Preheat the oven to 350 degrees. Butter the bottom of a 9-inch springform pan. Cut a circle of parchment or wax paper to fit the bottom of the pan, put it in the pan, and butter it.

In a microwave-safe bowl melt the butter and chocolate chips together in the microwave about 2 minutes, or until melted, stirring every 20 seconds. Or melt it in a heatproof bowl set over a saucepan of barely simmering water, stirring occasionally; the bottom of the bowl should not touch the water. Whisk together the sugar, cocoa powder, instant espresso, and salt, and add to the chocolate mixture. Add the eggs and vanilla and mix well. Pour the batter into the prepared pan.

Serves 10 to 12

Bake the cake for 45 minutes. Let cool in the pan. When the cake is completely cool, remove the outer ring from the pan, lift the cake off the bottom of the pan with a large spatula, peel off the parchment or wax paper, and transfer to a serving plate. The cake can be made ahead, covered with plastic wrap, and refrigerated for up to 2 days.

Pound Cake

Like the perfect pair of jeans, pound cake is a must-have staple. Delicious on its own, it can also be dolled up with berries and cream, topped with ice cream, cut into chunks and dipped into warm dark fudge sauce, or toasted for breakfast.

Makes one 9 × 5-inch loaf

16 tablespoons (2 sticks) unsalted butter, at room temperature

1 cup sugar

3 large eggs

1½ teaspoons pure vanilla extract

1¾ cups sweet rice flour blend

2 teaspoons baking powder

¼ teaspoon kosher or fine sea salt

½ cup whole milk, at room temperature

Preheat the oven to 350 degrees. Spray a 9 × 5-inch loaf pan lightly with gluten-free, nonstick cooking spray.

In the bowl of an electric mixer fitted with the paddle attachment, cream the butter and sugar on medium-high speed for 5 minutes until it is fluffy. Turn the speed to low. Add the eggs, one at a time, mixing well and scraping down the sides of the bowl with a spatula after each addition. Add the vanilla.

In a separate large mixing bowl, whisk together the sweet rice flour blend, baking powder, and salt. With the mixer on low speed, add the flour mixture and milk to the creamed butter starting with half of the flour mixture, then the milk, then the rest of the flour mixture. Mix until just combined. Remove the bowl from the mixer and scrape down the sides and bottom of the bowl well with a large spatula. Pour the batter into the prepared pan.

Bake the cake for 50 to 60 minutes, or until the top is golden brown and a toothpick inserted in the center comes out clean. Check the cake after 40 minutes. If the top is browning too quickly, place a sheet of foil loosely over it to protect it. When the cake is done, remove it from the oven, let cool in pan for a full 15 minutes, then remove it from the pan and transfer to a wire rack to finish cooling.

The cake will keep, well wrapped in plastic wrap, in the refrigerator for at least 3 days.

Party Cake

ꙮꙮꙮꙮꙮꙮꙮꙮꙮꙮꙮꙮꙮꙮ

Everyone needs a great basic cake that can be filled and frosted for special occasions. I realize that we can now buy gluten-free cake mixes in a box, but trust me, this homemade classic yellow cake is worth the extra bit of effort.

You can frost and fill this cake any way you wish, but I like to spread the layers with seedless raspberry or blackberry jam and frost it with dark chocolate frosting. You will need about 1 cup of jam to layer the cake.

The cake layers can be baked ahead and then refrigerated or frozen. Wrap tightly in plastic wrap after cooling to keep them fresh.

12 tablespoons (1½ sticks)
    unsalted butter, at room
    temperature
1½ cups sugar
4 large eggs, at room temperature
1½ teaspoons pure vanilla
    extract

2¾ cups sweet rice flour
    blend
1 tablespoon baking powder
¾ teaspoon kosher or fine sea
    salt
¾ cup whole milk, at room
    temperature

Preheat the oven to 350 degrees. Lightly spray two 9-inch cake pans with gluten-free, nonstick cooking spray and line the bottom of each with a round of parchment paper cut to fit.

In the bowl of an electric mixer fitted with the paddle attachment, cream the butter and sugar on medium speed until smooth, about 2 minutes. Turn the speed to low, and add the eggs, one at a time, mixing well until each egg is fully incorporated, and scraping down the sides of the bowl with a spatula after each addition. Add the vanilla and mix well.

In a separate large mixing bowl, whisk together the sweet rice flour blend, baking powder, and salt. With the mixer on low speed, add the flour mixture and milk to the creamed butter starting with one-third of the flour mixture, then half the milk, half the remaining flour mixture, the rest of the milk, and the rest of the flour mixture. Mix until just combined. Remove the bowl from the mixer and scrape down the sides and bottom of the bowl well with a large spatula. Divide the batter evenly between the prepared pans, and smooth the tops with a small spatula.

Bake the cake layers 30 to 35 minutes, or until springy on the top and a toothpick inserted in the center comes out clean. Run a knife around the edge of each pan and allow the cake layers to cool in the pans for 30 minutes, then remove from the pans and transfer to a wire rack to cool completely. Peel off the parchment paper.

To assemble the cake, cut each layer in half horizontally, using a long, serrated knife, making four layers. Place one layer on a serving plate cut side up, and tuck four strips of parchment paper under the cake layer to keep the plate clean. Spread on a layer of frosting. If using jam, spread about ⅓ cup of jam on the next layer on the outside then flip it over, and place jam side down on the frosting. Frost the top of that layer and repeat with the remaining layers.

Using an offset spatula, spread a thin layer of frosting around the sides and on the top of the cake to catch the crumbs. Let set for about 5 minutes, then frost the cake, swirling or smoothing the frosting as desired. Carefully remove the strips of parchment paper.

Apple Almond Cake

- Grain-free
- Dairy-free

Serves 10 to 12

This grain- and dairy-free cake has a moist texture and surprisingly buttery taste. The cinnamon-almond topping provides a nice crunch. It is the perfect dessert for a casual dinner, with an afternoon cup of coffee, or even for breakfast. The cake is best served warm but is equally delicious cold.

CAKE

1³/₄ cups sugar

1 heaping cup unsweetened applesauce

8 large eggs, at room temperature

3¹/₄ cups almond meal

1 tablespoon freshly squeezed lemon juice

TOPPING

³/₄ cup sliced almonds

3 tablespoons sugar

1 tablespoon ground cinnamon

Preheat the oven to 350 degrees. Spray a 10-inch springform pan with gluten-free, nonstick cooking spray and line the bottom with a circle of parchment paper cut to fit.

Put the sugar into a food processor and process for 1 minute. Add the rest of the cake ingredients and process to a puree. Using a large spatula, scrape the batter into the prepared pan.

Sprinkle the sliced almonds all over the top of the cake. Mix together the 3 tablespoons of granulated sugar and ground cinnamon and sprinkle evenly all over the almonds.

Bake the cake for about 35 to 45 minutes, or until a toothpick inserted in the center comes out clean. Let cool in the pan about 10 minutes, then remove the sides of the pan and remove the cake from the bottom of the pan. Peel off the parchment paper. Place on a serving plate.

Cornmeal Strawberry Shortcake

This cake was inspired by one of my favorite cookbook authors, Ina Garten. I converted her Strawberry Country Cake to a gluten-free cake and added some cornmeal for an even more rustic feel.

The recipe makes two 8-inch cakes, so I always pop the extra one in the freezer to have on hand for unexpected entertaining!

CAKE

12 tablespoons (1½ sticks) unsalted butter, at room temperature

2 cups sugar

4 extra-large eggs, at room temperature

¾ cup sour cream, at room temperature

1 teaspoon finely grated orange zest

½ teaspoon pure vanilla extract

1½ cups sweet rice flour blend

½ cup cornmeal

¼ cup cornstarch

½ teaspoon kosher or fine sea salt

1 teaspoon baking soda

TOPPING AND FILLING (ENOUGH FOR 1 CAKE)

1 cup heavy whipping cream

2 tablespoons sugar

½ teaspoon pure vanilla extract

1 pint fresh strawberries, hulled and sliced

Preheat the oven to 350 degrees. Spray two 8-inch cake pans with gluten-free, nonstick cooking spray.

In the bowl of an electric mixer fitted with the paddle attachment, cream together the butter and sugar on high speed until light and fluffy, about 3 minutes. Turn the speed to low, and add the eggs, one at a time, mixing well until each egg is fully incorporated, and scraping down the sides of the bowl with a spatula after each addition. Add the sour cream, orange zest, and vanilla and mix well.

In a separate large mixing bowl, whisk together the sweet rice flour blend, cornmeal, cornstarch, salt, and baking soda. With the mixer on low speed,

Makes two
8-inch cakes,
each serving
6 to 8

slowly add the flour mixture to the butter mixture and combine just until smooth. Scrape down sides and bottom of the bowl to ensure that the batter is well mixed.

Divide the batter evenly between the prepared pans. Rap the pans on the counter three times to smooth out the batter. Bake the cakes for 40 to 45 minutes, or until a toothpick inserted in the center comes out clean. Let the cakes cool in the pans for 30 minutes, then remove from the pans and transfer to a wire rack to cool completely.

If freezing one of the cakes, once completely cool, wrap it well in plastic wrap and freeze for up to 6 months. Thaw for about 1 hour at room temperature before serving.

To make the filling for *one* cake, whip the cream until firm and add the sugar and vanilla. Cut one of the cakes in half horizontally with a long, serrated knife. Place the bottom half cut side up on a serving plate, spread half the whipped cream over the cake, and scatter on most of the sliced strawberries. Cover with the top slice of cake cut side down, spread on the remaining whipped cream, and garnish with the rest of the strawberries.

No-bake Chocolate Truffle Cake

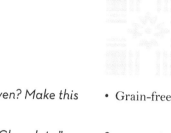

How great is it that you can make a cake without turning on the oven? Make this the night before you plan to serve it.

My friend Derek told me I should call this cake "Genocide by Chocolate," so be forewarned—it is very rich! Unless you want your guests dropping into a chocolate coma, serve thin slices.

• Grain-free

Serves 10 to 12

CAKE

3 cups semisweet chocolate chips

2 tablespoons instant espresso powder

2¼ cups heavy whipping cream

2 teaspoons pure vanilla extract

TOPPING

1 cup heavy whipping cream

2 teaspoons sugar

Unsweetened cocoa powder for garnish

Spray an 8-inch springform pan with gluten-free, nonstick cooking spray and line with plastic wrap.

In a microwave-safe bowl, melt the chocolate in the microwave for about 2 minutes or until melted, stirring every 20 seconds. Or melt it in a heatproof bowl set over a saucepan of barely simmering water, stirring until melted; the bottom of the bowl should not touch the water. Add the espresso powder to the melted chocolate and stir well. Set aside to cool.

Beat the cream and vanilla until soft peaks form. Stir half the whipped cream into the chocolate-coffee mixture and then fold in the remaining cream. Pour the mixture into the prepared pan and swirl the top with an offset spatula to make a pretty pattern. Refrigerate overnight to firm up.

Just before serving prepare the topping. Whip the cream with the sugar until stiff peaks form.

Cut the cake into thin slices, top with a dollop of whipped cream, and dust some cocoa powder on top by putting the cocoa powder in a small wire strainer and tapping it lightly over the cream.

Cakes and Cupcakes

Almond Cranberry Bundt Cake

Fresh cranberries give this moist, sweet cake just the perfect hint of tartness. This is a lovely dessert to make during the holidays when cranberries are in season.

This cake keeps well in the refrigerator for several days and freezes beautifully, wrapped tightly in plastic wrap.

4 tablespoons (½ stick) unsalted
    butter, at room temperature
    plus more for preparing the pan
8 ounces pure almond paste (not
    tart filling or marzipan)
1 cup granulated sugar
4 large eggs, at room temperature
½ teaspoon pure vanilla extract
½ teaspoon pure almond extract
1½ cups sweet rice flour blend
    plus more for preparing the pan

1½ teaspoons baking powder
½ teaspoon kosher or
    fine sea salt
¼ cup whole milk, at room
    temperature
1½ cups fresh cranberries,
    rinsed, dried, and coarsely
    chopped
Confectioners' sugar for dusting

Preheat the oven to 350 degrees. Butter a 10-cup bundt pan and sprinkle with some sweet rice flour blend. Tap out the excess flour.

In the bowl of an electric mixer fitted with the paddle attachment, cream the butter and the almond paste together on medium speed until smooth, about 2 minutes. Add the sugar and continue to beat until very light and fluffy, about 3 minutes more. Turn the speed to low, and add the eggs, one at a time, mixing well until each egg is fully incorporated, and scraping down the sides of the bowl with a spatula after each addition. Add the vanilla and almond extracts and mix well.

In a separate large mixing bowl, whisk together the sweet rice flour blend, baking powder, and salt. With the mixer on low speed, add half the flour mix-

ture to the butter mixture, then the milk, then the rest of the flour, and mix well. Turn off the mixer and scrape down the sides and bottom of the bowl well with a large spatula. Fold in the chopped cranberries. Pour the batter into the prepared pan and smooth the top with a spatula. Rap the pan three times on the counter to settle the batter.

Bake the cake for 40 to 50 minutes, or until a toothpick inserted in the center comes out clean. Let the cake cool in the pan for 30 minutes, then invert it onto a wire rack, remove the pan, and let cool completely.

Sprinkle with confectioners' sugar, tapped through a fine strainer.

Triple Lemon Pound Cake

Lemon cake soaked with lemon syrup topped with lemon glaze!—this is a lemon lover's dream cake. Great for brunch, afternoon tea, or after a casual summer dinner—this cake is as versatile as it is delicious.

CAKE
8 tablespoons (1 stick) unsalted butter, at room temperature

1 cup granulated sugar

3 large eggs, at room temperature

¼ cup lemon zest, finely grated (from 3 to 4 lemons)

1½ cups sweet rice flour blend

½ teaspoon baking powder

½ teaspoon baking soda

½ teaspoon kosher or fine sea salt

2 tablespoons freshly squeezed lemon juice

¼ cup plus 2 tablespoons buttermilk, at room temperature

½ teaspoon pure vanilla extract

SYRUP
¼ cup granulated sugar

¼ cup freshly squeezed lemon juice

GLAZE
1 cup confectioners' sugar, sifted

1 to 2 tablespoons freshly squeezed lemon juice

Finely grated lemon zest for garnish, optional

Preheat the oven to 350 degrees. Spray a 9×5-inch loaf pan lightly with gluten-free, nonstick cooking spray.

In the bowl of an electric mixer fitted with the paddle attachment, cream the butter and sugar on medium speed until very light and fluffy, about 5 minutes. Turn the speed to low, and add the eggs, one at a time, mixing well until each egg is incorporated, and scraping down the sides of the bowl with a spatula after each addition. Add the lemon zest and mix well.

In a separate large mixing bowl, whisk together the sweet rice flour blend, baking powder, baking soda, and salt. In another small bowl, stir together the lemon juice with the buttermilk and the vanilla. With the mixer on low speed, add the flour and buttermilk mixtures to the creamed butter, starting with half the flour, then the buttermilk, and finally the rest of the flour. Mix until just combined. Remove the bowl from the mixer and scrape down the sides and bottom of the bowl well with a large spatula. Pour the batter into the prepared pan and smooth the top with the spatula.

Bake the cake for 35 to 55 minutes, or until a toothpick inserted in the center comes out clean.

While the cake is baking make the syrup. Combine the sugar and lemon juice together in a small saucepan and cook over low heat until the sugar is dissolved.

When the cake is done, let it cool for 10 minutes in the pan, then remove from the pan and transfer to a wire rack, placed over a rimmed baking sheet. Spoon the syrup evenly over the cake and let it soak in while the cake continues to cool. Let the cake cool completely.

While the cake is cooling, make the glaze. In a small mixing bowl, combine the confectioners' sugar with 1 tablespoon lemon juice and whisk together. You want a thick but pourable consistency; add more lemon juice as needed. Pour over the top of the cake letting it drizzle down the sides. Place the cake on a serving platter. Garnish with finely grated lemon zest, if desired.

Milla Plum Cakes

- Grain-free
- Dairy-free

My youngest granddaughter's name is Milla Plum. Milla means apples in Greek, so of course I had to come up with an apple-plum cake in her honor.

These upside-down cakes are baked in individual ramekins and are best served warm, topped with vanilla ice cream. Milla always likes extra ice cream on hers—thank-you very much!

CARAMEL TOPPING

1½ cups sugar

¼ cup water

6 large plums, each cut into
   6 pieces

CAKE BATTER

1 cup sugar

¾ cup unsweetened applesauce

4 large eggs, at room temperature

1 teaspoon pure vanilla extract

Pinch of kosher or fine sea salt

1¾ cups almond meal

Vanilla ice cream for serving,
   optional

Lightly spray six 1¼-cup ramekins with gluten-free, nonstick cooking spray.

Prepare the caramel topping. Combine the sugar and water in a heavy saucepan and set over medium heat. Stir to dissolve the sugar. Increase the heat to medium-high and bring the mixture to a boil. Continue to cook, without stirring, until the mixture has turned a deep amber color, about 8 minutes.

Carefully divide the hot mixture among the prepared ramekins. Rotate each ramekin to cover the bottom with the caramel. Being careful not to burn your fingers, arrange 6 plum slices on top of the caramel in each ramekin. Work quickly or the caramel will harden too much.

Preheat the oven to 350 degrees.

Prepare the cake batter. Put the sugar into a food processor and process for

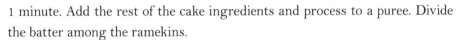

1 minute. Add the rest of the cake ingredients and process to a puree. Divide the batter among the ramekins.

Bake the cakes for 30 to 40 minutes, or until a toothpick inserted in the center of the cakes comes out clean.

Run a small knife around each cake to loosen. Invert the cakes onto individual plates and serve warm, topped with vanilla ice cream, if desired.

Chocolate Marmalade Cake

- Grain-free
- Dairy-free

Serves 6 to 8

*This cake came from both inspiration and desperation. The inspiration was pro-
vided by Nigella Lawson's Chocolate Orange Cake from her wonderful cookbook Feast in which she boils a couple oranges for two hours, pulverizes them,
and adds the mixture to an almond-based chocolate batter. The desperation
came from not allowing adequate time to cook and cool the oranges. My solution? Use orange marmalade.*

*The orange really complements the chocolate, and the rind in the marmalade
gives the cake an almost fruitcake-like feel (but oh so much better than fruitcake!).*

1 1/4 cups sugar

One 12-ounce jar orange
   marmalade

6 large eggs

1 heaping teaspoon baking
   powder

1/2 teaspoon baking soda

2 cups ground almond meal

1/2 cup unsweetened cocoa
   powder

Fine strips of orange zest for
   garnish, optional

Preheat the oven to 350 degrees. Spray an 8-inch springform pan with gluten-
free, nonstick cooking spray and line the bottom with a circle of parchment
paper cut to fit.

Put the granulated sugar into a food processor and process for 1 minute.
Add the rest of the cake ingredients and process until well blended. With a
large spatula, scrape the batter into the prepared pan.

Bake the cake for 50 to 60 minutes, or until a toothpick inserted in the center comes out clean. You should check the cake after about 40 minutes because
sometimes the top gets too browned before the cake is fully baked. If the top is
browning too quickly, cover the cake loosely with a piece of aluminum foil.

Let the cake cool completely in the pan placed on a wire rack. When completely cool, remove from the pan.

Place on a serving plate. Garnish with fine strips of orange zest, if you wish.

Molten Lava Cakes

Make these cakes for your next dinner party and your guests will treat you like a rock star.

How long you bake these will depend on how gooey you want the centers to be. The cakes should be firm on the edges but still jiggly in the center. Whatever you do, resist the urge to overbake the cakes; after all, lava cakes without the eruptions of warm, velvety chocolate are really just chocolate cakes.

The batter can be prepared ahead of time, poured into ramekins, and refrigerated until baking time. Take the ramekins out of the refrigerator and let stand at room temperature for about 30 minutes before putting them in the oven. In the unlikely event you have leftovers, a few seconds in the microwave will restore the volcanic center.

1¼ cups semisweet chocolate chips

10 tablespoons (1 stick plus 2 tablespoons) unsalted butter

½ cup sweet rice flour blend

1½ cups confectioners' sugar

3 large eggs

3 large egg yolks

1 teaspoon pure vanilla extract

2 tablespoons Kahlúa or other coffee-flavored liqueur

Whipped cream, ice cream, sliced berries, or confectioners' sugar for garnish, optional

Preheat the oven to 350 degrees. Spray eight 4-ounce ramekins or large muffin cups with gluten-free nonstick cooking spray.

Place the chocolate chips and butter in a large microwave-safe mixing bowl and microwave for about 3 minutes, or until the butter has liquefied and most of the chocolate is melted, stirring every 20 seconds. Or melt it in a heatproof bowl set over a saucepan of barely simmering water, stirring occasionally; the bottom of the bowl should not touch the water. Stir the melted butter and chocolate until smooth. Let cool slightly.

Stir in the sweet rice flour blend and the confectioners' sugar. Add the eggs,

Makes 8
individual
cakes

egg yolks, vanilla, and coffee liqueur and blend well; you may have to use a whisk for this. Divide the batter among the prepared ramekins or muffin cups.

Bake the cakes for 9 to 12 minutes, or until the edges are firm but the center is still jiggly (almost runny but not quite).

Remove the cakes from the oven, let cool for a minute or two, and run a knife around the edges of the ramekins or muffin cups to loosen the cakes. To unmold, invert the ramekins onto individual serving plates. If using a muffin pan, invert the pan onto a large, flat surface (like a cutting board) and gently lift the cakes onto serving plates using a thin, flexible spatula. Serve immediately topped with whipped cream, ice cream, berries, or a dusting of confectioners' sugar.

Mexican Chocolate Cake with Cinnamon Whipped Cream

If you have ever had Mexican hot chocolate you will understand how enticing the mixture of spice and chocolate can be. With the warmth of the cinnamon and the slight kick from the ancho chili powder, this flourless chocolate cake is kicked up from merely amazing to exotically fabulous. It is rich, so serve thin slices.

• Grain-free

CAKE

16 tablespoons (2 sticks) unsalted butter, cut into pieces plus more for preparing the pan

1½ cups semisweet chocolate chips

1¼ cups sugar

1 cup unsweetened cocoa powder, sifted

1 tablespoon instant espresso powder (or instant coffee granules)

Pinch of kosher or fine sea salt

2 tablespoons ancho chili powder

½ teaspoon ground cinnamon

6 large eggs

1 teaspoon pure vanilla extract

CINNAMON WHIPPED CREAM

1 cup heavy whipping cream

2 teaspoons sugar

½ teaspoon ground cinnamon

Preheat the oven to 350 degrees. Butter the bottom of a 9-inch springform pan. Cut a circle of parchment or wax paper to fit the bottom of the pan, put it in the pan, and butter it.

In a microwave-safe bowl, melt the butter and chocolate chips together in a microwave, about 2 minutes, or until melted, stirring every 20 seconds. Or melt it in a heatproof bowl set over a saucepan of barely simmering water, stirring occasionally; the bottom of the bowl should not touch the water. Mix together the sugar, cocoa powder, instant espresso or coffee crystals, salt, ancho chili powder, and cinnamon and add to the chocolate mixture. Add the eggs and vanilla and mix well. Pour the batter into the prepared pan.

Serves 10 to 12

Bake the cake for 45 minutes. Let the cake cool in the pan for about 10 minutes or so. You can remove from the pan and finish cooling it on a wire rack, or not; I often just let it cool in the pan. Remove the outer ring from the pan, lift the cake off the bottom of the pan with a large spatula, peel off the paper, and transfer to a serving plate.

Just before serving, whip the cream, sugar, and cinnamon together until thick and stiff but not dry. Serve the cinnamon whipped cream atop thin slices of the cake.

Mango Sticky Rice Cake

Growing up as an Air Force brat my family lived in Southeast Asia, the south-eastern United States, and California. I wanted to come up with a gluten-free cake that would embrace my pan-cultural upbringing and decided on a takeoff of Filipino rice cake, Thai sticky rice, and good old American pineapple upside-down cake.

- Dairy-free (if using nondairy butter substitute)

4 tablespoons (½ stick) butter or nondairy butter substitute plus more for preparing pan

1 cup firmly packed brown sugar plus 1 tablespoon

2 mangoes, peeled and sliced lengthwise into about ¼-inch slices

1½ cups sweet rice (mochi, pearl, or sushi rice)

1½ cups water

One 13.5-ounce can coconut milk

Pinch of kosher or fine sea salt

Preheat the oven to 350 degrees. Prepare a 9-inch round cake pan by greasing the bottom and sides liberally with butter or nondairy butter substitute. Sprinkle the 1 tablespoon of brown sugar over the bottom of the pan in an even layer. Lay the sliced mango on top of the brown sugar layer in a nice spiral pattern.

Put the rice in a large glass bowl and cover with enough water to come about 1 inch over the top of the rice. Soak the rice for at least 1 hour. Strain off the water, rinse with cold running water, and put back into the bowl with 1½ cups fresh water. Cover tightly with plastic wrap. Microwave on high for 5 minutes. Stir the rice thoroughly and return it to the microwave for another 5 minutes. Stir again; the rice should be tender, cooked through, and sticky. If not, microwave it for another 3 minutes and check again. When done, let the rice stand, covered, for 5 minutes. Alternatively you can cook the soaked rice in a rice cooker.

Serves 8 to 10

While the rice is cooking, shake the can of coconut milk well, and add to a saucepan with ¼ cup brown sugar and the salt. Cook until almost boiling over medium heat; do not cook it over too high a heat or it will curdle. When all the sugar is dissolved and the mixture is very hot, pour it over the cooked rice, stir well, and let sit for at least 5 minutes.

Melt the butter or nondairy butter substitute over medium heat with ¾ cup of the brown sugar until it forms a thick caramel. Gently pour the caramel over the mango slices in the cake pan. Add the rice mixture and press down to pack it well into the pan. Smooth out the top with a spatula. Place the cake pan on a sheet pan to catch any caramel that may bubble over.

Bake the cake in the oven for 20 to 25 minutes, or until the rice is lightly browned and the caramel is hot and bubbling. Let cool for 5 minutes, and then run a knife around the pan to loosen. Invert the cake onto a serving plate and let cool. The longer you cool it the easier it is to slice.

Cranberry Upside-Down Cake

Topped with a jewel-like crown of glistening cranberries, this cake is a beautiful addition to any holiday table or dessert buffet.

Even though the cake is inverted onto a serving platter after baking I bake it in a springform pan as a regular cake pan isn't deep enough. Just be sure to wrap the outside of your pan with foil first or you will have the pleasure of cleaning your oven as well as serving this showstopping cake.

• Grain-free

TOPPING

5 tablespoons ($^1\!/_2$ stick plus 1 tablespoon) unsalted butter

$^2\!/_3$ cup firmly packed light brown sugar

Pinch of kosher or fine sea salt

$2^1\!/_2$ cups fresh cranberries, washed and dried

CAKE

8 ounces pure almond paste (not tart filling or marzipan)

8 tablespoons (1 stick) unsalted butter, at room temperature

1 cup sugar

4 large eggs, at room temperature

1 teaspoon pure vanilla extract

2 teaspoons finely grated orange zest

$3^1\!/_4$ cups blanched almond flour

$^1\!/_2$ teaspoon baking soda

$^1\!/_2$ teaspoon kosher or fine sea salt

$^1\!/_4$ cup freshly squeezed orange juice

Preheat the oven to 350 degrees. Spray a 10-inch springform pan with gluten-free, nonstick cooking spray, and wrap the outside with two sheets of aluminum foil, pinching it tightly around the bottom. Set aside.

Prepare the topping. In a small, heavy saucepan, cook the butter, brown sugar, and salt over medium heat until the butter is melted, the sugar is dissolved, and the mixture comes to a slow boil. Pour the mixture into the prepared pan, spreading it evenly, and top with the cranberries. Even out the

cranberries and gently push them into the brown sugar mixture. Set aside and let cool slightly while preparing the cake.

In the bowl of an electric mixer fitted with the paddle attachment, cream the almond paste with the butter on medium-high speed until smooth, about 2 minutes. Add the sugar and beat until light and fluffy, about 2 minutes more. Turn the speed to low, and add the eggs, one at a time, mixing well until each egg is fully incorporated and scraping down the sides of the bowl with a spatula after each addition. Add the vanilla and orange zest and mix well.

In a separate large mixing bowl, whisk together the almond flour, baking soda, and salt. With the mixer on low speed, add half the almond flour mixture, then the orange juice, and finally the rest of the almond flour mixture and mix well. With a large spatula, scrape down the sides and bottom of the bowl well to make sure all the ingredients are well combined. Pour the batter over the cranberries, and place the pan on a baking sheet.

Bake the cake for 35 to 45 minutes, or until it is golden brown and a toothpick inserted into the center comes out clean. Let cool for 5 minutes, then invert the pan onto a serving platter. Let the pan stay on the cake for 2 to 3 minutes, then remove it. Let the cake cool completely.

This cake is best served slightly warm or at room temperature and is especially good served with a dollop of lightly sweetened whipped cream.

Chocolate Chestnut Cake

• Grain-free

This is a fabulous, grain-free holiday cake. If you are so inclined you could certainly use about three-quarters of a pound of fresh chestnuts that you have roasted and peeled, but honestly that is just too much work for me especially during the busy holiday season.

I rarely can get the ganache to be perfectly smooth around the sides of the cake so I simply wrap a piece of ribbon around it for presentation. It looks pretty and hides any imperfections.

For a dairy-free version, make the ganache with coconut milk and fold melted chocolate into dairy-free whipped topping instead of making the chocolate cream filling.

CAKE

14 to 15 ounces plain jarred
    chestnuts (not the glazed,
    sweetened type)

4 large eggs, separated, plus 1
    additional egg white

3/4 cup granulated sugar

2 teaspoons pure vanilla extract
    (or use dark rum)

1 cup blanched almond flour

CHOCOLATE CREAM FILLING

3 ounces semisweet chocolate

1 cup heavy whipping cream

1/2 cup apricot jam or preserves

1 recipe Chocolate Ganache
    (page 84)

Confectioners' sugar for garnish,
    optional

Preheat the oven to 350 degrees. Spray a 10-inch springform pan with gluten-free, nonstick cooking spray and line the bottom with a circle of parchment paper cut to fit.

Reserve 1 chestnut for the top of the cake as a decoration. Place the rest of the chestnuts in a food processor and process in long pulses until they have turned into a fine meal. Do not process so long that it turns into a paste.

In the bowl of an electric mixer fitted with the whisk attachment, beat the egg whites at high speed until stiff peaks form.

In another mixing bowl, beat the egg yolks and sugar until very light and fluffy, about 3 minutes. Gradually add the ground chestnuts and vanilla extract (or rum) and mix well. Fold in the almond flour and beaten egg whites. Pour the batter into the prepared pan.

Bake the cake for 10 minutes, reduce the heat to 325 degrees, and continue to bake for 40 to 50 minutes, or until a toothpick inserted into the center comes out clean. Let cool for 5 minutes, then remove the outer ring of the springform pan. Let the cake cool completely. Remove the bottom of the springform pan and the parchment paper. While cake is cooling, make the chocolate cream filling, the apricot jam glaze, and the ganache.

To make the chocolate cream filling, in a microwave-safe bowl, melt the chocolate in the microwave for 1 to 2 minutes stirring every 20 seconds until melted. Or melt it in a heatproof bowl placed over a saucepan of barely simmering water, stirring occasionally; the bottom of the bowl should not touch the water. Let cool.

Whip the cream until stiff peaks form and fold in the cooled chocolate. Set aside.

Melt the apricot jam in a small saucepan. Slice the cooled cake horizontally into two layers using a long, serrated knife. Spread the cut sides of each layer with the apricot jam. Place one of the cake layers, jam side up, on a wire rack that has been placed over a rimmed baking sheet. Top the jam with the chocolate cream filling, and place the other layer, jam side down, on top. Gently press the two layers together, removing any chocolate cream filling that has seeped out the sides of the cake with a spatula.

Make the ganache according to the recipe directions. Spread half the ganache over the top and sides of the cake. Let set for 5 to 10 minutes, then pour the rest of the ganache over the cake, making sure it flows down the sides of

the cake. You can help it spread with an offset spatula. Let set about 15 minutes, or until the ganache has hardened. Carefully, using a long, wide spatula, place the cake on a serving plate.

Dust a little confectioners' sugar over the reserved chestnut, if desired, and place off center on top of the cake.

Burnt Almond Cake

I developed this cake for my birthday this year. I wanted a cake that was light, not overly sweet with almond overtones, and one that would look pretty without a lot of fussy decorating.

While this recipe may appear complex at first glance, realize that no individual step is difficult and all the components can be prepared ahead. The sponge cake can be made two days ahead and refrigerated, or it can be frozen for as long as two months if wrapped well in plastic wrap. Thaw at room temperature before assembling. The praline powder can be made a couple weeks ahead and stored in an airtight container at room temperature. The pastry cream will hold up for a day or two in the refrigerator, but I don't recommend whipping the cream and folding it into the pastry cream until a few hours prior to serving.

For less auspicious occasions, slice one layer of the dairy-free sponge cake in half horizontally, spread with jam, and dust with confectioners' sugar or top with chocolate ganache.

ALMOND SPONGE CAKE

8 large eggs

1 cup granulated sugar

2 cups sweet rice flour blend

2 teaspoons pure vanilla extract

1 teaspoon pure almond extract

Pinch of kosher or fine sea salt

ALMOND SIMPLE SYRUP

1/4 cup granulated sugar

1/4 cup water

A few drops pure almond extract
    or 1/3 cup almond liqueur such
    as Amaretto

PRALINE POWDER

2 1/2 cups slivered almonds

2 cups granulated sugar

1/2 cup water

ALMOND CREAM

1 recipe Pastry Cream
    (page 188)

2 teaspoons pure almond
    extract, use divided

1 tablespoon cool water

1/2 teaspoon unflavored gelatin

1 1/4 cups heavy whipping cream

1 tablespoon confectioners' sugar

Prepare the almond sponge cake. Preheat the oven to 350 degrees. Lightly spray two 8-inch cake pans with gluten-free, nonstick cooking spray, dust with some sweet rice flour blend, tapping out the excess, and line the bottom of each pan with a circle of parchment paper cut to fit.

Fill a large mixing bowl of an electric mixer with hot tap water and place the eggs in the hot water for 5 minutes. Remove the eggs and pour out the water. Separate the eggs, placing the yolks in the warm bowl and the whites in another large mixing bowl. Add ¾ cup of the sugar to the yolks. Fit the mixer with the paddle attachment and beat the yolks and sugar on medium-high speed for about 30 seconds. Turn the mixer off, scrape down the sides and bottom of the bowl, then turn the speed back to medium-high and mix for 5 minutes. The mixture should triple in volume and be a very light yellow color.

Turn the speed to low, and very gradually add the sweet rice flour blend about ¼ cup at a time, making sure the flour is mixed in before making the next addition. (As you add more and more flour, the mixture will have a harder time absorbing the flour.) Once all the flour is added, remove the bowl from the mixer, add the vanilla and almond extracts, and blend by hand using a large spatula to ensure all the flour is absorbed and the extracts are well incorporated.

In a large clean mixing bowl of an electric mixer fitted with the whisk attachment, beat the egg whites, remaining ¼ cup sugar, and salt on high speed until very firm, slightly dry peaks form. Stir one-third of the whites into the yolk mixture then fold in the rest in two stages, folding until the mixture is no longer streaky. Divide the batter between the prepared pans and immediately place in the preheated oven.

Bake the cake layers for 25 to 30 minutes, or until the cakes barely spring back when touched in the center, and the tops have lightly browned. Let cool in the pans for 5 minutes, then run a knife around the edge of each pan and invert the cakes onto a wire rack, peel off the parchment paper, and let cool for at least 1 hour.

Prepare the simple syrup. Combine the sugar and water in a small saucepan, stir to combine, and bring to a boil. Take off the heat and stir in a few drops of almond extract. Simple syrup can be made several days ahead of time and refrigerated, or you can skip this step and use Amaretto to moisten the cakes.

Make the praline powder. Preheat the oven to 350 degrees. Line a baking sheet with parchment paper.

Lay the almond slivers on another baking sheet in a single layer. Toast in the oven for 10 to 15 minutes, or until they are warm and fragrant.

Meanwhile, put the sugar and water in a large saucepan, stir to combine, and bring to a boil over medium-high heat. Once the mixture starts to boil, do not stir any longer. You can gently swirl the pan, if necessary, to make sure the mixture colors evenly. Cook for about 10 minutes, or until the mixture turns an amber color. Take off the heat and stir in the warm almonds.

Put the mixture into the prepared baking pan and spread with a spatula into an even layer. *Be very careful!* This mixture is screaming hot so it is a good idea to wear an oven mitt while doing this. Let the praline harden completely.

Once the praline has hardened, break the brittle into pieces and place in a food processor. Process with long pulses until the mixture is a coarse powder. The praline can be made two weeks ahead and stored in an airtight container at room temperature.

To make the almond cream, begin by preparing the basic pastry cream recipe using 2 teaspoons pure vanilla extract and 1 teaspoon pure almond extract instead of the tablespoon of vanilla extract called for in the original recipe. Cover with plastic wrap, pressing it directly on the surface of the cream to prevent a skin from forming, and refrigerate until cold. The almond cream can be made 2 days ahead.

Place the cool water in a small microwave-safe bowl and sprinkle the gelatin over it. Let sit for 5 minutes. Microwave on the highest power for 10 seconds to dissolve the gelatin.

In the bowl of an electric mixer fitted with the whisk attachment, whip the cream on high speed with 1 teaspoon almond extract and the confectioners' sugar until soft peaks start to form. Pour in the melted gelatin all at once and continue beating until stiff peaks form. Whisk the chilled pastry cream and then fold in the whipped cream until well blended.

To assemble the cake, cut each cake in half horizontally using a long, serrated knife, making four layers. Brush each cut side with some almond simple syrup or Amaretto. Place one layer cut side up on a serving plate, and tuck four strips of parchment paper under the cake to keep the plate clean. Spread about 1 cup of almond cream on top almost to the edges, sprinkle on a generous handful of the praline powder, and top with another cake layer. Repeat with the remaining layers. Frost the cake with the remaining almond cream, smoothing the sides. Press praline powder into the sides of the cake using the parchment paper to help you. Gently swirl the top of the cake and sprinkle more praline powder on top. Remove parchment paper strips. Refrigerate the cake for at least half an hour or up to several hours.

Most likely you will have praline powder left over; it is delicious sprinkled on ice cream!

Black Forest Cupcakes

These cupcakes were inspired by my dear German friend Christiane who would make her grandmother's Black Forest Cake for birthdays and other special events.

With the combo of chocolate, whipped cream, and cherries these cupcakes are not only delicious but they are as beautiful as Christiane.

CUPCAKES

8 tablespoons (1 stick) unsalted
    butter, at room temperature

1 1/2 cups granulated sugar

2 large eggs, at room temperature

1 teaspoon pure vanilla extract

1 2/3 cups sweet rice flour blend

2/3 cup unsweetened cocoa
    powder

2 teaspoons baking powder

1 teaspoon kosher or fine sea salt

1 1/2 cups whole milk

One 14.5-ounce can tart red
    cherries, drained

One 10-ounce jar maraschino
    cherries, drained and liquid
    reserved

TOPPING

1 cup heavy whipping cream

1 cup confectioners' sugar

1/2 teaspoon pure vanilla extract

Grated chocolate for garnish

Preheat the oven to 350 degrees. Insert paper liners into 24 standard-size muffin cups.

In the bowl of an electric mixer fitted with the paddle attachment, cream the butter and sugar on medium speed until very light and fluffy, about 5 minutes. Turn the speed to low, and add the eggs, one at a time, mixing well until each egg is fully incorporated, and scraping down the sides of the bowl with a spatula after each addition. Add the vanilla and mix well.

In a separate large mixing bowl, whisk together the sweet rice flour blend, cocoa powder, baking powder, and salt.

With the mixer on low speed, add the flour mixture and milk to the creamed butter starting with one-third of the flour mixture, then half of the milk, half the remaining flour mixture, the rest of the milk, and the rest of the flour mixture. Mix until just combined. Remove the bowl from the mixer and scrape down the sides and bottom of the bowl well with a large spatula.

Spoon 2 tablespoons of batter into each prepared muffin cup, add 3 of the red tart cherries to each cup then top with 2 more tablespoons of batter, dividing the batter among the prepared pans.

Bake the cupcakes for 20 to 25 minutes, or until springy on the top. Allow to cool in pan for about 5 minutes.

With a toothpick, poke about 6 or 8 holes in each cupcake. Spoon about 1 teaspoon of the reserved maraschino cherry liquid onto each cupcake and let it soak in. Remove the cupcakes from the pans and transfer to a wire rack to cool completely.

Just before serving, make the topping. Whip the cream in a large bowl until soft peaks form. Add the confectioners' sugar, vanilla, and 1 tablespoon of the reserved maraschino cherry juice. Beat until stiff.

Frost the cupcakes with the topping and garnish with a maraschino cherry and some grated chocolate.

Coconut Cupcakes

These cupcakes always receive rave reviews from the gluten-free and gluten eaters alike. A non-gluten-free friend of mine from New York once told me she would gladly stand in line and pay $5.00 for one of these cupcakes!

I make these as big, oversized cupcakes but if you prefer to make yours smaller then fill the baking liners only two-thirds full. This will yield you closer to 36 cupcakes but, personally, I feel that the generous size of these cupcakes adds to their charm.

CUPCAKES

1 tablespoon freshly squeezed lemon juice

1 cup coconut milk (shake can well before measuring)

³/₄ pound (3 sticks) unsalted butter, at room temperature

2 cups granulated sugar

6 large eggs, at room temperature

1¹/₂ teaspoons pure vanilla extract

1¹/₂ teaspoons pure almond extract

3 cups sweet rice flour blend

1 teaspoon baking powder

¹/₂ teaspoon baking soda

¹/₂ teaspoon kosher or fine sea salt

14 ounces sweetened, shredded coconut

FROSTING

1 pound cream cheese, at room temperature

³/₄ pound unsalted butter, at room temperature

Pinch of kosher or fine sea salt

1 teaspoon pure vanilla extract

¹/₂ teaspoon pure almond extract

1¹/₂ pounds confectioners' sugar

Preheat the oven to 325 degrees. Lightly spray 24 large-size muffin cups with gluten-free, nonstick cooking spray and insert paper liners in each cup.

Stir the lemon juice into the coconut milk and let set for 5 minutes. Do not become concerned if it starts to look curdled.

In the bowl of an electric mixer fitted with the paddle attachment, cream the butter and sugar on medium speed until very light and fluffy, about 5 minutes. Turn the speed to low, and add the eggs, one at a time, mixing well until each egg is fully incorporated, and scraping down the sides of the bowl with a spatula after each addition. Add the vanilla and almond extracts and mix well.

In a separate large mixing bowl, whisk together the sweet rice flour blend, baking powder, baking soda, and salt. With the mixer on low speed, add the flour mixture and coconut milk mixture to the creamed butter starting with one-third of the flour mixture, then half the coconut milk mixture, half the remaining flour mixture, the rest of the coconut milk mixture, and the rest of the flour mixture. Mix until just combined. Remove the bowl from the mixer and scrape down the sides and bottom of the bowl well with a large spatula. Fold in half of the coconut. Fill each prepared muffin cup to the top with batter. Rap the pans on counter three times to settle the batter.

Bake the cupcakes for 25 to 30 minutes, rotating the pans halfway through the baking time, until springy on the top and a toothpick inserted in the center comes out clean. Allow the cupcakes to cool in the pan for 10 minutes, then remove from the pans and transfer to a wire rack to cool completely. You may have to run a small offset spatula gently around the edges of the cupcakes to get them out of the pan without breaking the tops.

While the cupcakes are baking and cooling, make the frosting. In the bowl of an electric mixer fitted with the paddle attachment, blend together the cream cheese, butter, salt, and vanilla and almond extracts on medium speed. Turn off the mixer. Sift in the confectioners' sugar, turn the mixer back on, and mix on low speed until smooth.

Put the frosting in the refrigerator to firm up while the cupcakes finish baking and cooling. When the cupcakes are completely cool, frost with the chilled frosting.

Makes 24 large cupcakes

Chocolate Ginger Bites

At the age of seventy my father, a widower, met Doris, a widow, and they fell in love. They proved to the world that it is never too late to find happiness.

Doris was the first person to introduce me to candied ginger covered with dark chocolate, a flavor combination I instantly found addictive. Whenever I make these mini cupcakes I think of Doris and the joy and contentment she gave my father.

6 tablespoons (³/₄ stick) unsalted butter, at room temperature

²/₃ cup granulated sugar

1 large egg, at room temperature

¹/₂ teaspoon pure vanilla extract

One 1-inch cube fresh ginger, peeled and finely grated

1¹/₄ cups sweet rice flour blend

1 teaspoon ground ginger

¹/₄ teaspoon baking powder

¹/₄ teaspoon baking soda

¹/₂ teaspoon kosher or fine sea salt

¹/₂ cup sour cream, at room temperature

¹/₄ cup crystallized ginger, finely chopped

1 recipe Chocolate Ganache (page 84)

Crystallized ginger for garnish

Preheat the oven to 350 degrees. Line 36 mini muffin cups with paper liners.

In the bowl of an electric mixer fitted with the paddle attachment, cream the butter and sugar on medium speed until light and fluffy, about 3 minutes. Turn the speed to low, add the egg, and mix well, scraping down the sides and bottom of the bowl with a spatula. Add the vanilla and grated fresh ginger and mix well.

In a separate large mixing bowl, whisk together the sweet rice flour blend, ground ginger, baking powder, baking soda, and salt. With the mixer on low speed, add the flour mixture and sour cream to the creamed butter starting with one-third of the flour mixture, then half the sour cream, half the remaining flour mixture, the rest of the sour cream, and the rest of the flour mixture. Mix until just combined. Remove the bowl from the mixer and scrape down the sides and bottom of the bowl well with a large spatula. Fold in the chopped, crystallized ginger. Fill the prepared muffin cups about three-quarters full with batter.

Bake the cupcakes for 17 to 20 minutes, or until the tops are springy and a toothpick inserted in the middle comes out clean. Allow the cupcakes to cool in the pans for 5 minutes, then remove from the pans and transfer to a wire rack to cool completely.

Prepare the ganache according to the recipe directions. When the cupcakes are cool, dip the tops into the chocolate ganache and let the ganache cool. Garnish the cupcakes with thin strips of crystallized ginger.

Makes 36 mini cupcakes

Lemon-Lime Cupcakes

These cupcakes have a dense base bursting with citrus and a sweet glaze topping. For some reason they seem very feminine to me and are the perfect complement to an afternoon tea party.

CUPCAKES

2 lemons, preferably organic

2 limes, preferably organic

8 tablespoons (1 stick) unsalted butter, at room temperature

1/2 cup granulated sugar

3 large eggs, at room temperature

1/2 teaspoon pure vanilla extract

1 cup plus 2 tablespoons sweet rice flour blend

1/2 teaspoon baking powder

Scant 1/2 teaspoon kosher or fine sea salt

GLAZE

1 1/2 cups confectioners' sugar, sifted

Candied Citrus Peels (page 126) for garnish, optional

Preheat the oven to 325 degrees. Insert paper liners into 12 standard-size muffin cups.

Finely zest the lemons and limes and mix together, reserving 1/4 teaspoon for the glaze. Juice the lemons and limes and mix together the juices. Measure out 3 tablespoons of the juice for the glaze. Reserve the rest for another use.

In the bowl of an electric mixer fitted with the paddle attachment, cream the butter and sugar on medium speed until very light and fluffy, about 5 minutes. Turn the speed to low, and add the eggs, one at a time, mixing well until each egg is fully incorporated, and scraping down the sides of the bowl with a spatula after each addition. Add the vanilla and lemon and lime zest (except for the 1/4 teaspoon reserved for the glaze) and mix well.

In a separate large mixing bowl, whisk together the sweet rice flour blend, baking powder, and salt. With the mixer on low speed, gradually add the flour mixture into the butter mixture. With a large spatula, scrape down the sides and bottom of the mixing bowl to ensure that the batter is well mixed. Divide the batter among the prepared muffin cups.

Makes 12 cupcakes

Bake the cupcakes for 20 to 25 minutes, or until springy on the top and a toothpick inserted in the center comes out clean. Allow the cupcakes to cool in the pan for 10 minutes, then remove from the pan and transfer to a wire rack to cool completely.

When the cupcakes are completely cooled, whisk together the confectioners' sugar, the reserved 3 tablespoons of citrus juice, and the reserved ¼ teaspoon of zest until completely smooth.

Set the rack with the cooled cupcakes on a rimmed baking sheet. Spoon the glaze onto the cupcakes and refrigerate until the glaze hardens, about half an hour.

Garnish with candied citrus peels, if desired.

Grain-free Chocolate Cupcakes

~~~~~~

- Grain-free
- Dairy-free
- Sugar-free

Makes 18
cupcakes

With no grain, dairy, or sugar there is just nothing bad for you in these cupcakes! They are the perfect everyday treat, especially for children you want to instill with good eating habits. Who knew healthy could taste so good?

CUPCAKES

3 large eggs, separated

$1/4$ cup grapeseed oil

$3/4$ cup light agave nectar

1 tablespoon pure vanilla extract

$2^1/_2$ cups blanched almond flour
(not almond meal)

$1/_2$ teaspoon kosher or fine sea salt

$1/_2$ teaspoon baking soda

$1/_4$ cup unsweetened cocoa
powder

1 recipe Marshmallow Frosting
(page 86)

Preheat the oven to 350 degrees. Line 18 standard muffin cups with paper liners.

In the bowl of an electric mixer fitted with the whisk attachment, whisk the egg yolks until they become a pale yellow, then whisk in the grapeseed oil, agave nectar, and vanilla.

In a clean bowl with a clean whisk, beat the egg whites until stiff peaks form. With a large spatula take one-fourth of the egg white mixture and mix into the egg yolks, then gently fold in the rest of the egg whites.

In a large mixing bowl, whisk together the almond flour, salt, baking soda, and cocoa powder, then gently fold the dry mixture into the egg mixture. Fill the prepared muffin cups two-thirds full with the batter.

Bake the cupcakes for 20 to 25 minutes, or until the tops are golden brown and a toothpick inserted in the center comes out clean.

Let the cupcakes cool in the pan for 15 minutes, then remove from the pan and transfer to a wire rack to cool completely.

While the cupcakes are baking and cooling, make the frosting.

When the cupcakes are completely cool, frost generously.

Eileen's New York Cheesecakelettes

I love New York Cheesecake but find it a bit too rich to eat a whole slice. These little cheesecakelettes solve that problem. I can eat as much or as little as I like, one bite at a time.

When I asked my friend Angie for her recipe to convert she said to make sure I let it be known this was not her recipe but her friend Eileen's. Thank you Eileen!

These taste best when they are made at least one day ahead so they are perfect for entertaining.

CRUST
1½ cups blanched almond flour

2 tablespoons granulated sugar

¼ cup honey

3 tablespoons unsalted butter, melted

¼ teaspoon kosher or fine sea salt

FILLING
16 ounces cream cheese, at room temperature

2 large eggs, at room temperature

½ heaping cup sugar

2 teaspoons fresh lemon juice

1 teaspoon pure vanilla extract

TOPPING
1 cup sour cream

2 tablespoons sugar

½ teaspoon pure vanilla extract

24 fresh blueberries

Preheat the oven to 350 degrees. Insert paper liners into 24 mini muffin cups.

Combine all the ingredients for the crust in a mixing bowl. Divide the mixture evenly among the prepared muffin cups.

In the bowl of an electric mixer fitted with the paddle attachment, beat the cream cheese on medium speed until smooth. Add the rest of the filling ingredients and mix well. Divide the filling evenly on top of the crusts. Bake the cheesecakelettes for 10 minutes, or until the filling is set but not dry looking. Leave the oven on. Let the cheesecakelettes cool in the pan for 10 minutes. Make the topping.

Makes 24 mini cheesecakes

Combine all the topping ingredients and whisk until smooth. Spoon on the cheesecakelettes after they have cooled for 10 minutes. Return them to the oven and bake for 3 minutes.

Keep the cheesecakelettes in the pan and let them cool to room temperature, then cover with plastic wrap, and refrigerate overnight (24 hours is even better).

Remove the cheesecakelettes from the pans and top with the fresh blueberries.

Flourless Marble Cupcakes

The chocolate part of these cupcakes is rich and fudgy, and the vanilla part is almost like cheesecake.

The cupcakes puff up when baking and then the centers sink when cooled, creating the perfect vessel for ice cream, whipped cream, berries, or any combination thereof.

I prefer to use a combination of bittersweet and semisweet chocolate but, by all means, you can use all bittersweet or all semisweet depending on how sweet you like your chocolate.

• Grain-free

CHOCOLATE BATTER

¾ cup bittersweet chocolate chips

¾ cup semisweet chocolate chips

10 tablespoons (1 stick plus 2 tablespoons) unsalted butter

3 large eggs

⅓ cup sugar

1 tablespoon Kahlúa or brewed espresso

1 teaspoon pure vanilla extract

Pinch of kosher or fine sea salt

VANILLA BATTER

8 ounces cream cheese, at room temperature

⅔ cup sugar

1 large egg

1 teaspoon pure vanilla extract

Preheat the oven to 300 degrees. Line 24 standard-size muffin cups with paper liners.

Prepare the chocolate batter. In a medium bowl, melt the chocolates and butter in the microwave for 2 to 3 minutes, stirring every 20 seconds. Or melt it in a heatproof bowl placed over a saucepan of barely simmering water, stirring occasionally; the bottom of the bowl should not touch the water. Let the chocolate cool slightly.

In the bowl of an electric mixer fitted with the whisk attachment, beat the

Cakes and Cupcakes

eggs, sugar, Kahlúa or espresso, vanilla, and salt at medium-high speed until pale and thick, about 4 minutes. Turn the speed to low, add the chocolate mixture gradually, and mix until well blended.

Prepare the vanilla batter. In the bowl of an electric mixer fitted with the paddle attachment, beat the cream cheese on medium speed until smooth. Add the sugar and mix until well blended and lump-free. Add the egg and vanilla and mix until just blended.

Divide half of the chocolate mixture evenly among the prepared muffin cups (about a heaping tablespoon in each). Spoon small spoonfuls of the vanilla and chocolate batters on top of the chocolate base—I usually do three spoonfuls of each batter alternately in each cup. With the tip of a small, sharp knife or a wooden skewer, gently swirl the batters together. Rap the pans three times on the counter to settle the batter.

Bake the cupcakes for 30 to 40 minutes, or until a toothpick inserted into the center comes out gooey but not liquid. The tops of the cupcakes will be puffed and the edges slightly cracked. Do not overbake. Allow the cupcakes to cool in pans for 10 minutes, then remove the pans and transfer to a wire rack to cool completely. The centers will sink as the cupcakes cool.

Red Velvet Cupcakes

I have no idea why someone once decided to dump a bunch of red food coloring into cake batter but red velvet cake is a Southern favorite. Some say the red velvet cake was invented in the 1950s by the chef of the Waldorf Astoria in New York but die-hard Southerners claim this unusual cake dates back to the Civil War and was originally colored with beets. Whatever the truth, I can tell you this—these cupcakes are always a hit around my house.

CUPCAKES

³/₄ pound (3 sticks) unsalted butter, at room temperature

2¹/₂ cups sugar

3 large eggs, at room temperature

1¹/₂ teaspoons pure vanilla extract

4 ounces red food coloring

3¹/₂ cups sweet rice flour blend

¹/₄ cup unsweetened cocoa powder

1¹/₂ teaspoons kosher or fine sea salt

1¹/₂ cups buttermilk

1¹/₂ teaspoons apple cider vinegar

1¹/₂ teaspoons baking soda

1 recipe Cream Cheese Frosting (page 83)

Unsweetened cocoa powder for dusting

Preheat the oven to 350 degrees. Insert paper liners into 24 standard-size muffin cups.

In the bowl of an electric mixer fitted with the paddle attachment, cream the butter and sugar on medium speed until very light and fluffy, about 5 minutes. Turn the speed to low, and add the eggs, one at a time, mixing well until each egg is fully incorporated, and scraping down the sides of the bowl with a spatula after each addition. Add the vanilla and red food coloring and mix well.

In a separate large mixing bowl, whisk together the sweet rice flour blend, cocoa powder, and salt.

With the mixer on low, add the flour mixture and buttermilk to the creamed butter starting with one-third of the flour mixture, then half the buttermilk, half the remaining flour mixture, the rest of the buttermilk, and the rest of the flour mixture. Mix until just combined. Remove the bowl from the mixer and scrape down the sides and bottom of the bowl well with a large spatula.

In a small bowl mix together the apple cider vinegar and the baking soda. Add to the batter and mix very well. Divide the batter among the muffin cups. Rap the pans on the counter three times to settle the batter.

Bake the cupcakes for 20 to 25 minutes, turning the pans halfway through the baking time, until springy on the top, and a toothpick inserted in the center comes out clean. Allow the cupcakes to cool in the pans for 10 minutes, then remove from the pans and transfer to a wire rack to cool completely.

While the cupcakes are baking and cooling make the frosting according to the recipe directions.

Once the cupcakes are completely cool, frost each cupcake generously. Put some unsweetened cocoa powder in a small strainer and dust a little over each cupcake.

Julian's Carrot Cupcakes

~~~~~~

When I first asked my then three-year-old grandson Julian if he would like some • Dairy-free
carrot cake he laughed hysterically and thought I was making a great joke. I real-
ized that since carrots were vegetables the idea of carrot cake was as funny to
him as say, string bean cake. He got over his prejudice and now carrot cakes,
especially carrot cupcakes, are his favorite.

To keep this recipe dairy-free, top with marshmallow frosting, or use a more
traditional cream cheese frosting if dairy is not an issue. Unfrosted these make
terrific lunch box snacks.

2 cups granulated sugar

1⅓ cups grapeseed (or other
    neutral-tasting vegetable) oil

1 teaspoon pure vanilla extract

2 tablespoons freshly squeezed
    orange juice

1 tablespoon freshly grated
    orange zest

4 large eggs, at room tempera-
    ture

2 cups sweet rice flour blend

2 teaspoons ground cinnamon

2 teaspoons baking powder

1 teaspoon baking soda

1½ teaspoons kosher or fine
    sea salt

1 pound carrots, grated (about
    3 cups)

1 cup raisins

1 cup walnuts, chopped

1 recipe Marshmallow Frosting
    (page 86) or Cream Cheese
    Frosting (page 83),
    optional

Preheat the oven to 350 degrees. Insert paper liners into 24 standard-size muffin cups.

In the bowl of an electric mixer fitted with the paddle attachment, beat together the sugar, oil, vanilla, orange juice, and zest on medium speed. Turn
speed down to low and add the eggs, one at a time, mixing well until each egg

Makes 24 cupcakes

is fully incorporated, and scraping down the sides of the bowl with a spatula after each addition.

In a separate large mixing bowl, whisk together the sweet rice flour blend, ground cinnamon, baking powder, baking soda, and salt.

With the mixer on low speed, add half the flour mixture to the wet ingredients. Add the carrots, raisins, and walnuts to the remaining flour mixture and toss well to coat. Add to the batter and mix well using a large spatula, and making sure to scrape down the sides and bottom of the bowl well. Divide the batter evenly among the prepared muffin cups. Tap the pans on the counter three times gently to settle the batter.

Bake the cupcakes for 35 to 45 minutes, rotating the pans halfway through the baking time, until a toothpick inserted in the center comes out clean. Cool for about 10 minutes in pans then remove from the pans and transfer to a wire rack to finish cooling. When completely cool, frost, if desired.

P.B. and J. Cupcakes

Every child deserves a cupcake to celebrate birthdays, soccer wins, and good grades even if they have food allergies.

Classic, kid-approved flavors—peanut butter and jelly—are sure to be a hit with the little ones in your life.

• Grain-free

CUPCAKES

4 large eggs, separated

½ teaspoon cream of tartar

Pinch of kosher or fine sea salt

3 tablespoons granulated sugar

¾ cup creamy peanut butter

3 tablespoons neutral-tasting vegetable oil

1 teaspoon pure vanilla extract

½ cup ground almonds (almond meal)

1 teaspoon baking soda

¼ cup good-quality strawberry jam

FROSTING

8 ounces cream cheese, at room temperature

12 tablespoons (1½ sticks) unsalted butter, at room temperature

1 teaspoon pure vanilla extract

1½ cups confectioners' sugar, sifted

3 heaping tablespoons good-quality strawberry jam

Preheat the oven to 350 degrees. Line 12 standard-size muffin cups with paper liners.

In the bowl of an electric mixer fitted with the whisk attachment, beat the egg whites with the cream of tartar and the salt until soft peaks form. With the mixer running, add the sugar, 1 tablespoon at a time, until stiff peaks form.

In a clean bowl, beat the egg yolks with the peanut butter, oil, and vanilla on high speed until very smooth. Add the ground almonds and baking soda and mix well. Add the beaten egg whites and mix in with a spatula or spoon until batter is no longer streaky.

Makes 12 cupcakes

Put about 2 scant tablespoons of batter in the bottom of each prepared muffin cup. Add 1 teaspoon of jam to each cupcake and top with the remaining batter.

Bake the cupcakes for 20 to 25 minutes until they have risen and are golden brown and springy to the touch. Cool in the pans for 10 minutes, and then remove from the pans and transfer to a wire rack to finish cooling.

While the cupcakes are baking and cooling, prepare the frosting. In the bowl of an electric mixer fitted with the paddle attachment, blend together the cream cheese, butter, and vanilla on medium speed. Turn the mixer off, and add the confectioners' sugar. Start the mixer again on low speed and blend in the sugar, increasing the speed to medium high and beating until the mixture is very smooth. Add the jam and mix until just combined.

When cupcakes are completely cool, frost with the strawberry–cream cheese frosting.

Mint Chip Cupcakes

Whenever we go out for ice cream, my husband always orders mint chip. I wanted to make a cupcake out of his favorite ice cream flavor combo for him. These are best made as mini cupcakes, that way you get the best frosting-to-cupcake ratio.

We got into a heated debate about the amount of mint extract to put in these cupcakes. I thought the recipe was perfect with 1 teaspoon, he preferred a more minty taste, 2 teaspoons. You should start with the lesser amount, tasting the batter as you go until the correct amount of mintiness is achieved for your tastes.

I prefer to chop the chocolate by hand as it gives a more authentic appearance but you can use chocolate chips if you don't feel up to the manual labor of chopping.

8 tablespoons (1 stick) butter, at room temperature

1 cup sugar

2 large eggs, at room temperature

1 teaspoon pure vanilla extract

1 to 2 teaspoons pure mint extract

3 cups sweet rice flour blend

1 tablespoon baking powder

1/4 teaspoon baking soda

1/2 teaspoon kosher or fine sea salt

1 1/2 cups buttermilk

5 or 6 drops of green food coloring

4 ounces bittersweet dark chocolate, chopped

1/2 recipe of Dark Chocolate Frosting (page 85), 1 recipe of Chocolate Swiss Buttercream (page 89), or 1 recipe of Chocolate Ganache (page 84)

Preheat the oven to 325 degrees. Insert paper liners into 36 to 40 mini muffin cups.

In the bowl of an electric mixer fitted with the paddle attachment, cream the butter and sugar on medium speed until light and fluffy, about 3 minutes.

Turn the speed to low, and add the eggs, one at a time, mixing well until each egg is fully incorporated, and scraping down the sides of the bowl with a spatula after each addition. Add the vanilla and mint extracts and mix well.

In a separate large mixing bowl, whisk together the sweet rice flour blend, baking powder, baking soda, and salt. With the mixer on low, add the flour mixture and buttermilk to the creamed butter starting with one-third of the flour mixture, then half the buttermilk, half the remaining flour mixture, the rest of the buttermilk mixture, and the rest of the flour mixture. Mix until just combined. Remove the bowl from mixer and scrape down the sides and bottom of the bowl well with a large spatula. Add the food coloring a couple drops at a time and mix in well until you get the color the shade of mint chip ice cream. Fold in the chopped chocolate. Fill the prepared muffin cups two-thirds full with the batter.

Bake the cupcakes for 12 to 17 minutes, or until the tops are springy to the touch and a toothpick inserted in the center comes out clean. Allow the cupcakes to cool in pans for 5 minutes then remove from the pans and transfer to a wire rack to cool completely.

Prepare chocolate frosting of your choice. For me the darker the better! When the cupcakes are completely cool, frost generously.

Bananas Foster Cupcakes

I got the idea for these cupcakes while dining with friends at a fancy steak house. Bananas Foster was the only gluten-free dessert they offered and I became obsessed with turning this classic dessert into a cupcake.

If you are brave, you can flame the rum in the bananas by carefully holding a long match to it but this step will be largely unappreciated unless you have an audience and the alcohol will burn off anyway.

If rum is not liquor you typically have on hand, those small airplane cocktail-size bottles can be purchased at most liquor stores for a dollar or two.

5 ripe but firm bananas

14 tablespoons (1³/₄ sticks) unsalted butter, at room temperature

¹/₃ cup firmly packed light brown sugar

2 tablespoons dark rum

³/₄ cup sugar

3 large eggs, at room temperature

1 teaspoon pure vanilla extract

2 cups sweet rice flour blend

¹/₂ teaspoon baking soda

1 teaspoon baking powder

¹/₂ teaspoon kosher or fine sea salt

¹/₄ cup buttermilk

Brown Sugar Cream Cheese Frosting (page 87)

Preheat the oven to 350 degrees. Line 16 to 18 standard-size muffin cups with paper liners.

Peel the bananas and slice them on the diagonal about ¼ inch thick. Melt 6 tablespoons (¾ stick) of the butter in a large skillet over medium heat. Add the brown sugar and cook, stirring constantly, until the mixture is well combined, about 2 minutes. Add the bananas and stir gently to coat. Add the rum, and flame it if you wish or just let it cook for another 2 minutes, or until the bananas start to caramelize. Be careful not to cook them too long or the bananas will become mushy. Set aside to cool. Reserve 16 to 18 banana slices for garnish.

In the bowl of an electric mixer fitted with the paddle attachment, cream the remaining 8 tablespoons (1 stick) butter and granulated sugar on medium speed until light and fluffy, about 3 minutes. Turn the speed to low, and add the eggs, one at a time, mixing well until each egg is fully incorporated, and scraping down the sides of the bowl with a spatula after each addition. Add the vanilla and the bananas and mix well.

In a separate large mixing bowl, whisk together the sweet rice flour blend, baking soda, baking powder, and salt. With the mixer on low speed, add the flour mixture and buttermilk to the creamed butter starting with half of the flour mixture, then the buttermilk, and then the rest of the flour mixture. Mix until just combined. Remove the bowl from the mixer and scrape down the sides and bottom of the bowl well with a large spatula.

Divide the batter evenly among the lined muffin cups. Rap the pans on the counter three times to settle the batter.

Bake the cupcakes for 20 to 25 minutes, rotating the pans halfway through the baking time, until springy on the top and a toothpick inserted in the center comes out clean. Allow the cupcakes to cool in the pans for 10 minutes, then remove from the pans and transfer to a wire rack to cool completely.

While the cupcakes are baking and cooling, prepare the frosting.

When the cupcakes are completely cool, frost each with the frosting and garnish with the reserved banana slices.

Peanut Butter–Filled Chocolate Cupcakes

Moist chocolate cupcakes filled with creamy peanut butter and topped with a rich chocolate ganache. It is hard to think of a better flavor combination than this!

Unfilled, this is a great basic chocolate cupcake, which you can frost as you wish.

CUPCAKES

1³/₄ cups sweet rice flour blend

1¹/₂ teaspoons baking soda

¹/₂ teaspoon kosher or fine sea salt

³/₄ cup unsweetened cocoa powder (not Dutch processed)

2 tablespoons instant espresso powder

¹/₂ cup boiling water

1 cup buttermilk

12 tablespoons (1¹/₂ sticks) unsalted butter, at room temperature

1¹/₂ cups granulated sugar

3 large eggs, at room temperature

1 teaspoon pure vanilla extract

FILLING

1 cup creamy peanut butter

4 tablespoons (¹/₂ stick) unsalted butter at room temperature

²/₃ cup confectioners' sugar

1 recipe Chocolate Ganache (page 84)

Preheat the oven to 350 degrees. Line 24 standard-size muffin cups with paper liners.

In a medium mixing bowl, whisk together the flour blend, baking soda, and salt.

Put the cocoa and instant espresso powder in a medium bowl and add the boiling water. Whisk until a smooth paste forms. Add the buttermilk and whisk until well combined.

In the bowl of an electric mixer fitted with the paddle attachment, cream together the butter with the granulated sugar on medium speed until light and fluffy, about 3 minutes. Turn the speed to low, and add the eggs one at a time, mixing well until each egg is fully incorporated, and scraping down the sides of the bowl with a spatula after each addition. Add the vanilla and mix well.

Add one-third of the flour mixture, half the buttermilk mixture, half the remaining flour mixture, the rest of the buttermilk, and finally the rest of the flour mixture. Mix until just combined. With a large spatula scrape down the sides and bottom of the bowl making sure the batter is well mixed. Scoop the batter into the lined muffin cups, filling each about two-thirds full.

Bake the cupcakes for 20 to 25 minutes, or until the top is springy and a toothpick inserted into the center comes out clean. Let the cupcakes cool in the pans for 10 minutes, and then remove from the pans and transfer to a wire rack to cool completely.

While the cupcakes are baking and cooling, prepare the filling. In the bowl of an electric mixer fitted with the paddle attachment, beat the peanut butter with the butter on medium speed until creamy. Turn off the mixer, sift in the confectioners' sugar. Turn the mixer on again, starting on low speed, and slowly increasing to medium speed, and beat until fluffy, about 2 minutes. Reserve 3 tablespoons of the filling to top the cupcakes and scoop the rest into a pastry bag fitted with a star tip, or into a small plastic storage bag and cut off ¼ inch of one corner.

Prepare the Chocolate Ganache according to the recipe directions.

When the cupcakes have cooled, take the end of a wooden spoon and gently press down in the center of each cupcake, wiggling the spoon back and forth to make a hole about 1 inch in diameter. Holding a cupcake in your hand, gently pipe the peanut butter filling into each cupcake, withdrawing the piping bag or plastic bag as you squeeze. Scrape any filling off the top of the cupcake so that the top is flat. Repeat with each cupcake.

Dip the top of each cupcake into the ganache, letting the excess drip back into the pan. Let set for 5 minutes, then dip again. Let stand for another 10 minutes until the ganache has firmed up.

Spoon the remaining 3 tablespoons of peanut butter filling into a pastry bag fitted with a star tip and pipe a little star garnish on top of each cupcake.

Makes 24 cupcakes

Very Vanilla Cupcakes

This is a great recipe for vanilla lovers. I normally make these using vanilla bean paste instead of vanilla extract; it intensifies the vanilla flavor and gives the cupcakes little specks of vanilla bean seeds throughout.

This is also a good basic recipe that can be transformed with different flavored extracts or the addition of chocolate chips. Frost it with any flavor your heart desires and, if you want to go all out, decorate with sprinkles, sanding sugar, or even candied fruit.

8 tablespoons (1 stick) unsalted
    butter, at room temperature
1 cup sugar
2 large eggs, at room tempera-
    ture
1 tablespoon vanilla bean paste
    or pure vanilla extract

3 cups sweet rice flour blend
1 tablespoon baking powder
$\frac{1}{4}$ teaspoon baking soda
$\frac{1}{2}$ teaspoon kosher or fine
    sea salt
$1\frac{1}{2}$ cups buttermilk

Preheat the oven to 325 degrees. Insert paper liners into 18 standard-size muffin cups.

In the bowl of an electric mixer fitted with the paddle attachment, cream the butter and sugar on medium speed until light and fluffy, about 3 minutes. Turn the speed to low, and add the eggs, one at a time, mixing well until each egg is fully incorporated, and scraping down the sides of the bowl with a spatula after each addition. Add the vanilla and mix well.

In a separate large mixing bowl, whisk together the sweet rice flour blend, baking powder, baking soda, and salt. With the mixer on low speed, add the flour mixture and buttermilk to the creamed butter starting with one-third of the flour mixture, then half the buttermilk, half the remaining flour mixture, the rest of the buttermilk mixture, and the rest of the flour mixture. Mix until just combined. Remove the bowl from mixer and scrape down the sides and

bottom of the bowl well with a large spatula. Fill the lined muffin cups two-thirds full with the batter.

Bake the cupcakes for 20 to 25 minutes, or until the tops are springy to the touch and a toothpick inserted in the center comes out clean. Allow the cupcakes to cool in the pans for 5 minutes, then remove from the pans and transfer to a wire rack to cool completely.

When the cupcakes are completely cool, frost and decorate as desired.

Makes about 18 cupcakes

Frostings

Cream Cheese Frosting

This is the perfect frosting for carrot cake, red velvet cupcakes, and a host of other desserts. It is quick to prepare and makes enough to frost twenty-four cupcakes or one large cake with a little extra for bowl licking! This frosting freezes well for up to two weeks in a covered container.

Makes about 4 cups frosting

12 ounces cream cheese, at room temperature

16 tablespoons (2 sticks) unsalted butter, at room temperature

$\frac{1}{4}$ teaspoon kosher or fine sea salt

1 teaspoon pure vanilla extract

1 pound confectioners' sugar

In the bowl of an electric mixer fitted with the paddle attachment, blend together the cream cheese, butter, salt, and vanilla extract on medium speed. Turn off the mixer. Sift in the confectioners' sugar, turn the mixer to low speed, and mix until smooth.

Chocolate Ganache

• Grain-free

Makes about
2 cups
ganache

Chocolate ganache is a classic and simple recipe that can be used in a number of ways. I like to replace half of the semisweet chocolate chips with bittersweet chocolate for a more intense chocolate flavor, or you can use all bittersweet chocolate for dark chocolate lovers.

The ganache can also be whipped and used as a more traditional frosting as opposed to a glaze. Let the ganache cool in the fridge for an hour and then whip until doubled in volume.

A dairy-free version can be made by using dairy-free chocolate chips and substituting coconut milk for the heavy whipping cream. Be sure to shake the can of coconut milk really well before measuring and heating.

**8 ounces semisweet or bitter-
sweet chocolate chips, or a
combination**

1 cup heavy whipping cream

Place the chocolate chips in a small, heatproof bowl. In a small saucepan, heat the cream over medium heat until it just comes to a boil. Pour the cream over the chocolate and let sit for 5 minutes, then whisk the cream and chocolate together until the mixture is shiny and smooth.

Ganache should be used soon after making it or it will start to harden up. If it becomes too hard to work with, gently reheat and stir until it comes back to the right consistency.

Dark Chocolate Frosting

This is a glossy, rich, dark, and delicious frosting that is not toothachingly sweet. It is also very easy to work with, smoothed or swirled on your cakes and cupcakes, and it can easily be piped. If you prefer a sweeter frosting use all semisweet chocolate instead of half bittersweet.

Makes about 5 cups frosting

8 ounces semisweet chocolate

8 ounces bittersweet chocolate

1/4 cup unsweetened cocoa powder

1/4 cup water

1 teaspoon pure vanilla extract

24 tablespoons (3 sticks) unsalted butter, at room temperature

1/2 cup confectioners' sugar

Pinch of kosher or fine sea salt

Combine the chocolates in a microwave-safe bowl and melt in the microwave for 2 to 3 minutes, stirring every 20 seconds, until melted. Or melt the chocolate in a heatproof bowl set over a saucepan of barely simmering water, stirring occasionally; the bottom of the bowl should not touch the water. Let the chocolate cool.

In a small saucepan over medium-high heat, combine the cocoa powder with the water and cook, stirring, until combined. Stir in the vanilla. Set aside to cool while mixing the butter and sugar.

Put the butter in the bowl of an electric mixer with paddle attachment, sift in the confectioners' sugar, and add the salt. Beat at medium-high speed until pale and fluffy, about 3 minutes. Reduce the speed to low and add the melted, cooled chocolate. Scrape down the sides of the bowl with a spatula, and then beat in the cocoa mixture until well combined.

Marshmallow Frosting

- Grain-free
- Dairy-free
- Sugar-free

Makes about
4½ cups
frosting

A great dairy- and sugar-free topping for cakes and cupcakes, this frosting is thick, glossy, and can easily be piped. Add a few drops of food coloring with the vanilla to turn this frosting into any shade you wish.

Leftover frosting can be refrigerated for a few days.

¾ cup light agave nectar
3 large egg whites

¾ teaspoon pure vanilla
extract

In a small heavy saucepan over medium-high heat, bring the agave nectar to a boil and continue to cook until it reaches 235 degrees on a candy thermometer. If you don't have a candy thermometer then cook the nectar until it starts to turn slightly amber in color and is thicker.

While the agave is cooking, put the egg whites in the bowl of an electric mixer fitted with the whisk attachment and whisk on high speed until firm peaks form. When the agave has reached the proper temperature, carefully pour the hot nectar into the egg whites with the mixer on low speed. After all the nectar is added, increase the speed to medium-high and continue beating until the frosting is completely cool, about 7 minutes; the frosting should be thick, glossy, and smooth. Add the vanilla and mix thoroughly.

Brown Sugar Cream Cheese Frosting

Use this frosting when you want a caramel flavor without all the work. This is great on Bananas Foster Cupcakes and a nice change for carrot cake.

• Grain-free

Makes about 2½ cups frosting

8 tablespoons (1 stick) unsalted butter, at room temperature

8 ounces cream cheese, at room temperature

1 cup firmly packed light brown sugar

¼ teaspoon kosher or fine sea salt

In the bowl of an electric mixer fitted with the paddle attachment, beat all the ingredients together on medium speed until smooth and creamy.

Swiss Buttercream Frosting

• Grain-free

Probably the most basic and versatile of frostings, this is one recipe you should have in your repertoire. It is very stable, easy to work with, can be piped and swirled, and is not as sweet as most buttercream frostings.

You can vary this basic recipe in an infinite number of ways by adding melted chocolate, extracts, instant espresso powder, fruit purees, or jam at the same time as you add the vanilla. You can also color it to your heart's content with food coloring, just be sure to add the food coloring gradually so you can control the final color.

This frosting keeps well in the refrigerator for 3 or 4 days and can even be frozen. Just bring it to room temperature and beat on low speed until smooth before using.

This recipe makes enough frosting for a two-layer cake or about twelve cupcakes, but it can easily be doubled.

2 large egg whites	16 tablespoons (2 sticks) unsalted
½ cup sugar	butter, cut into tablespoon-size
Pinch of kosher or fine sea salt	pieces, at room temperature
	1 teaspoon pure vanilla extract

In a heatproof bowl of a stand mixer, combine the egg whites, sugar, and salt. Place over a saucepan containing an inch or two of simmering water; the bottom of the mixing bowl should not touch the hot water. Whisk constantly, either by hand or with a handheld mixer, until the mixture feels warm to the touch and the sugar is dissolved, about 2 minutes. Test this by rubbing a bit of the mixture between your forefinger and thumb. It should be smooth and no longer gritty. This will take about two minutes.

Attach the bowl to the mixer fitted with the whisk attachment and beat until the mixture is glossy, fluffy, and completely cool, about 10 minutes. With the mixer on medium-low speed, add the butter a few tablespoons at a time

Simply . . . Gluten-free Desserts

88

mixing well after each addition. Once the butter has been fully incorporated, add the vanilla and mix well. With a spatula, scrape down the sides and bottom of the bowl and stir the frosting for a minute or two to knock out the air bubbles; it should be completely smooth. If the frosting starts to curdle or separate after adding the butter, don't worry. Just keep beating until it is smooth again.

VARIATIONS

Very Vanilla Swiss Buttercream: In place of the vanilla extract use 2 teaspoons of vanilla bean paste. This will give you a stronger vanilla flavor and those lovely little brown specks from the vanilla bean seeds.

Chocolate Swiss Buttercream: Fold in 2 to 4 ounces of melted and cooled semisweet or bittersweet chocolate, or a combination of the two (depending on how chocolaty you like it) after you have added the vanilla extract.

Coffee Swiss Buttercream: Add a tablespoon of instant espresso powder with the vanilla extract.

Mocha Swiss Buttercream: Add 2 to 4 ounces melted and cooled chocolate along with 1 tablespoon instant espresso powder.

Fruit Swiss Buttercream: Add 4 ounces of either fresh fruit or fruit puree with the vanilla extract. If using fresh fruit, it is best to use soft fruit like berries or bananas. Do not overmix.

Mint Swiss Buttercream: Add ¼ to ½ teaspoon of pure mint extract with the vanilla. Start with a little and add more to taste slowly to avoid a toothpaste flavor.

Cookies, Candies, and Bars

Mocha Macaroons

Macaroons exemplify my philosophy of gluten-free eating and cooking. They are naturally and simply gluten-free cookies. They require no flour, just a mixture of egg whites and nut meal or coconut.

These Mocha Macaroons are positively addictive—crunchy around the edges and chewy in the middle with rich chocolate flavor through and through.

- Grain-free
- Dairy-free

Makes 24 cookies

2 large egg whites
1½ cups confectioners' sugar
2 cups ground almond meal
3 tablespoons unsweetened
  cocoa powder

1 tablespoon instant espresso
  powder or instant coffee
  granules
Pinch of kosher or fine sea salt
1 teaspoon vanilla extract

Preheat the oven to 400 degrees. Line two baking sheets with either parchment paper or silicone baking mats.

Put all the ingredients in a mixing bowl and mix until well blended. If you have a sticky, gooey, chocolaty mess, then it's perfect.

Wet your hands with water, and pull up balls the size of a small walnut, or use a 1-tablespoon ice cream scoop. Place the balls on the prepared pans, leaving at least 1 inch between each cookie. You will probably have to re-wet your hands several times.

Bake the macaroons for 11 minutes. They will still seem a bit squishy when done but they harden up a little as they cool, and you want the insides chewy. Don't worry if the bottoms of the cookies look a bit sticky. Let cool on the baking sheets for 1 or 2 minutes, then transfer to a wire rack to finish cooling.

Chocolate Chunk Coconut Macaroons

• Grain-free

Makes about
28 cookies

I first made these cookies for my friend Shannon who is a coconut addict. She asked me if I could make a cookie similar to the base of her favorite restaurant dish, which contained coconut and chocolate chunks. I called her and told her they were in the oven. She was at my house in five minutes flat, and popped one in her mouth almost the second they came out of the oven. The sublime look on her face told me they hit the mark.

It is best to use good quality chocolate and roughly chop it into chunks as opposed to using chocolate chips, but chocolate chips will do in a pinch.

1 tablespoon sugar

2½ cups sweetened flaked coconut

2 large egg whites, lightly beaten with a fork

1 teaspoon pure vanilla extract

Pinch of kosher or fine sea salt

½ cup coarsely chopped semi-sweet chocolate

Preheat the oven to 325 degrees. Line baking sheets with either parchment paper or silicone baking mats.

In a large mixing bowl, mix all ingredients together making sure everything is completely combined. The easiest way to do this is to use your hands.

Wet your hands with water and form 1½ tablespoons of the mixture into a loose haystack and place on the prepared baking sheets. Repeat with the remaining mixture, spacing them about 1 inch apart.

Bake the macaroons for 15 to 20 minutes, rotating the pan halfway through the baking time, until golden brown. Let cool 5 minutes on the baking sheets, then transfer, with a spatula, to a wire rack to cool completely.

Praline Macaroons

My Auntie Eileen is a lovely, gracious woman with an infectious laugh who embodies southern hospitality. She also happens to make the world's best pralines. It was with her in mind that I came up with these cookies. Not as sweet as their candy counterpart, the pecans are the star of this show.

- Grain-free
- Dairy-free

Makes 36 to 48 cookies depending on size

2 large egg whites
Pinch of kosher or fine sea salt
¾ cup plus 2 teaspoons firmly packed light brown sugar

1½ cups plus 2 tablespoons medium to finely ground pecans
1½ teaspoons pure vanilla extract

Preheat the oven to 325 degrees. Line baking sheets with parchment paper or silicone baking mats.

In the bowl of an electric mixer fitted with the whisk attachment, beat the egg whites and salt on high speed until stiff peaks start to form. Add the ¾ cup brown sugar gradually, and continue beating for 5 minutes; the mixture will be very thick. Fold in the 1½ cups of ground pecans and the vanilla with a large spatula, making sure they are well combined; the batter will be very thick and sticky.

Using a tablespoon or small, 1-tablespoon ice cream scoop, drop mounds of the mixture onto the prepared sheets, spacing them about 2 inches apart.

Combine the 2 teaspoons of brown sugar with the remaining 2 tablespoons of ground pecans and mix. Sprinkle a pinch of the mixture on top of each macaroon and very gently press the mixture lightly into the top.

Bake the macaroons, for 15 to 17 minutes, rotating the baking pans halfway through the baking time, until they are set and slightly cracked. Let cool on the baking sheets for 5 minutes, then transfer to a wire rack to finish cooling.

Meringues

〰〰〰〰〰〰〰〰〰〰〰〰〰

- Grain-free
- Dairy-free

I think that the sheer brilliance behind cooking often goes overlooked. The person who discovered that whipping egg whites with sugar and baking them would result in such bliss was, to my thinking, a genius on the scale of Einstein or Edison.

As if it weren't enough that these cookies are melt-in-your-mouth delicious, they are not only gluten-, grain-, and dairy- free but fat-free as well. So go ahead and indulge in a little mouthful of heaven!

For an extra indulgence dip the meringues in some chocolate ganache. Of course that blows the whole fat free thing right out the window.

4 large egg whites	½ teaspoon pure vanilla extract
1 cup granulated sugar	½ recipe Chocolate Ganache
Pinch of cream of tartar	(page 84)

Preheat the oven to 175 degrees. Line baking sheets with either parchment paper or silicone baking mats.

Put the egg whites, sugar, and cream of tartar in a heatproof mixing bowl. Set the bowl over a saucepan of barely simmering water. Cook, whisking constantly, until the sugar has dissolved completely and the mixture is warm, about 3 or 4 minutes. To make sure the sugar is properly dissolved, rub a bit of the mixture between your thumb and forefinger; it should feel smooth and not gritty. When it is no longer gritty, the sugar is dissolved.

Remove the mixing bowl from the pan of simmering water and, using an electric mixer (with whisk attachment or beaters), beat the mixture starting on low speed and increasing to high, until stiff, glossy peaks form, about 10 minutes. Add the vanilla and mix well.

Transfer the mixture to a pastry bag fitted with a star tip and pipe into stars, fingers, or any other shape your heart desires onto the prepared baking sheets, spacing the meringues about 1 inch apart.

Bake the meringues for about 2 hours; they should lift off the parchment paper or silicone baking mat easily and should be firm and dry.

Meringues absorb moisture from the air and can become soggy so make sure you store them in an airtight container if you are going to eat them later.

If desired, the meringues can be dipped into chocolate ganache. Prepare ½ recipe of the ganache according to the recipe directions. Dip the meringues in the ganache and then set on a wire rack to let the ganache firm up. Double dipping is okay, too, just let set for 5 minutes between dippings.

Makes about 48 cookies

Pignoli Cookies

- Grain-free
- Dairy-free

Makes approximately 36 cookies

Specialties of Sicily, these Italian cookies are a favorite at Christmastime. Topped with pignoli, or pine nuts (the edible seeds from pine trees), these delectable cookies look deceptively plain but are packed with almondy goodness.

My son Colin says they remind him of an almond croissant, one of the things we miss from our gluten-eating days.

One 8-ounce can of pure almond paste (not tart filling or marzipan)

1 cup sugar

Pinch of kosher or fine sea salt

2 large egg whites

¹⁄₄ cup pine (pignoli) nuts

Preheat the oven to 350 degrees. Line two baking sheets with parchment paper or silicone baking mats.

Break the almond paste into small pieces and put into the bowl of a food processor. Process until almost smooth. With the processor running, gradually add the sugar through the feed tube. Turn off the processor, add the salt and egg whites, and then process until it turns into a batter.

Using a tablespoon or a small, 1-tablespoon ice cream scoop, drop the batter in mounds onto the prepared baking sheets, spacing them 2 inches apart. Press a few pine nuts onto each cookie.

Bake the cookies for approximately 15 minutes, or until they are firm and lightly browned. Let cool on the baking sheets for 5 minutes, then transfer to a wire rack to cool completely.

Amaretti

Legend has it that these cookies were invented by a pair of young lovers in the early 1700s and presented to the Cardinal of Milan upon his visit to Saronno. The Cardinal was so entranced by the cookies he blessed the couple and the cookies became a local favorite. The original amaretti recipe contains apricot kernels instead of the almonds.

   Serve these crispy, delicate cookies with coffee or a glass of wine, or crumble over ice cream. However you enjoy them I think you will agree that these cookies are indeed worthy of a blessing.

- Dairy-free

Makes about 24 cookies depending on size

1³/₄ cups sliced almonds	2 large egg whites, at room
1 cup confectioners' sugar	temperature
Pinch of kosher or fine sea	¹/₂ teaspoon pure almond extract
salt	¹/₄ teaspoon pure vanilla extract

Preheat the oven to 350 degrees. Line the baking sheets with parchment paper or silicone baking mats.

   Lay the almonds on a rimmed baking sheet in a single layer. Toast the nuts in the oven for 8 to 10 minutes, or until they are warm and fragrant. Set aside to cool. Leave the oven on.

   Process the cooled, toasted almonds, confectioners' sugar, and salt together in a food processor until they are finely ground.

   In the bowl of an electric mixer fitted with the whisk attachment, beat the egg whites on high speed until stiff peaks form. Gently fold the almond mixture into the egg whites. Fold in the almond and vanilla extracts.

   Using a tablespoon or small, 1-tablespoon ice cream scoop, drop the batter in mounds onto the prepared baking sheets, spacing them about 2 inches apart.

   Bake the cookies for 12 to 17 minutes, or until they are firm to the touch and golden brown. Let cool on the baking sheets for 5 minutes, then transfer to a wire rack to finish cooling.

Baci di Dama

• Grain-free

Baci di Dama *means Lady's Kisses in Italian. These flourless cookies are made with ground hazelnuts and filled with melted chocolate. Ground almonds can easily be substituted for the hazelnuts.*

The cookie is delicious all by itself, delicate and crispy on the outside, and chewy and marshmallowy on the inside like a nut macaroon. My husband actually prefers to eat them individually without sandwiching the chocolate between them.

If you are good at piping you can pipe the batter into little kisses, but I find it easier to make drop cookies using a small, tablespoon-size ice cream scoop. My cookies are a little larger than your typical Lady's Kisses, so maybe I should re-name them Lady's Smooches.

COOKIE	FILLING
2 large egg whites	3/4 cup semisweet chocolate
Pinch of kosher or fine sea salt	chips
1 cup sugar	1/2 teaspoon solid vegetable
1 teaspoon pure vanilla extract	shortening
1 1/2 cups medium to finely ground	
hazelnuts or almonds	

Preheat the oven to 325 degrees. Line baking sheets with parchment paper or silicone baking mats.

In the bowl of an electric mixer fitted with the whisk attachment, beat the egg whites and salt on high speed until stiff peaks form. Add the sugar gradually and continue beating until the egg whites are very thick, 2 to 3 minutes more. Add the vanilla and mix well. Stir in the nuts with a large spatula, making sure they are well combined. The batter will be very thick and sticky.

Using a tablespoon or small, 1-tablespoon ice cream scoop, drop mounds onto the prepared baking sheets, spacing them about 2 inches apart.

Bake the cookies for 15 to 17 minutes, rotating the baking pans halfway through the baking time, until they are set and slightly cracked. Let cool on the baking sheets for 5 minutes, then transfer to a wire rack to finish cooling. When the cookies have cooled make the filling.

Place the chocolate chips in a microwave-safe bowl and microwave on high for 1 to 2 minutes, or until melted, stirring every 20 seconds. Or melt the chocolate in a heatproof bowl set over a saucepan of barely simmering water, stirring occasionally; the bottom of the bowl should not touch the water. Add the shortening and stir until melted, and continue stirring until the chocolate is very smooth and glossy.

Spoon some chocolate filling onto the flat side of one cookie, place another cookie flat side down on the chocolate, and gently press the cookies together until some of the chocolate oozes out slightly. Place the cookies on a wire rack and let the chocolate set. Repeat with the remaining cookies and filling.

Makes about 24 cookies depending on size

Peanut Butter Cookies

- Grain-free
- Dairy-free

Makes about
24 cookies

These are the simplest of gluten-free desserts and a great cookie to make with kids. No mixers or other special equipment are needed, just a bowl and a spoon.

For those with peanut allergies, sunflower and almond butter work equally well, just make sure to stir the almond butter before using to incorporate any oil that may have risen to the top.

1 cup creamy peanut butter
1 cup sugar plus more for rolling
   the cookies in
1 large egg, lightly beaten with a
   fork

1 teaspoon baking powder
1 teaspoon vanilla extract

Preheat the oven to 350 degrees. Line baking sheets with either parchment paper or silicone baking mats.

In a large bowl mix the peanut butter with the 1 cup of sugar, using a wooden spoon. Stir until well blended. Add the egg, baking powder, and vanilla and stir well. Pour some additional sugar in a small bowl. Scoop out 1 tablespoon of the dough and roll it into a ball. Roll the dough ball in some of the remaining sugar and place on the prepared baking sheets. Repeat with the remaining dough, spacing the cookies 2 inches apart.

Using a dinner fork, first stick the tines of the fork in sugar and then gently press the tines down on each dough ball to flatten. Turn the fork 90 degrees and gently press again to make the traditional crosshatch markings of a peanut butter cookie.

Bake the cookies for 10 minutes. Remove from the oven and let cool on the baking sheets for 5 minutes. Then, with a spatula, gently transfer the cookies to a wire rack to finish cooling.

Lemon Sugar Cookies

Around the holidays we always make a big production of baking and decorating cookies. This recipe is perfect for cut-out cookies. The subtle lemon flavor cuts the sweetness slightly, making them appealing to adults and children alike.

Make extra dough and freeze it to have the convenience of those gluten-filled, prepackaged sugar cookie doughs you can buy in the grocery store. Just thaw in the refrigerator for a few hours prior to using.

The icing dries hard and shiny and the colors stay nice and bright.

COOKIES

8 tablespoons (1 stick) unsalted butter, at room temperature

1 cup granulated sugar

1 large egg, at room temperature

1 teaspoon pure vanilla extract

Zest of 1 lemon, finely grated (about 1 tablespoon, loosely packed)

2 tablespoons freshly squeezed lemon juice

2 cups sweet rice flour blend plus more for dusting

½ teaspoon baking powder

¼ teaspoon kosher or fine sea salt

ICING

2 cups confectioners' sugar

4 teaspoons freshly squeezed lemon juice

6 to 8 teaspoons light corn syrup

Food coloring

In the bowl of an electric mixer fitted with the paddle attachment, cream the butter and sugar on medium speed until smooth, about 2 minutes. Turn the speed to low, add the egg, vanilla, lemon zest, and lemon juice, and mix well.

In a separate large mixing bowl, whisk together the sweet rice flour blend, baking powder, and salt. Turn the speed to low, add the sweet rice flour mixture to the butter mixture, and mix well. Shape the dough into two flat disks, wrap with plastic wrap, and refrigerate for at least 1 hour. The dough can also be frozen at this point for future use.

**Makes about
24 cookies**

Preheat the oven to 350 degrees. Line baking sheets with either parchment paper or silicone baking mats.

Lay a piece of wax or parchment paper on a work surface and sprinkle it with some sweet rice flour blend. Place 1 dough disk on top, sprinkle with more sweet rice flour blend, and top with another piece of wax or parchment paper. Roll out the dough to a thickness of about ¼ inch. Just before the dough is rolled to the desired thickness, remove the top layer of wax paper, sprinkle a little more flour blend over the top of the dough, and then flip the dough over, wax paper and all. Remove the top layer of wax paper, sprinkle with a little more flour, and do your final roll or two. This will make it easier to remove the cookies once cut.

Cut out cookies into the desired shapes and place on the prepared baking sheets, spacing them about 1 inch apart. Brush off any excess flour. To keep the edges of the cookies sharp, refrigerate them for 15 minutes before putting them in the preheated oven. If you do not plan to ice the cookies, then sprinkle them with sugar before baking. Repeat with the remaining dough disk. Left-over dough can be re-rolled once; gather up the scraps, form into a disk, and refrigerate for at least 30 minutes before rolling.

Bake the cookies for about 10 minutes. Do not let the cookies brown. Let cool on the baking sheets for 10 minutes, then, using a spatula, transfer to a wire rack to cool completely.

Prepare the icing. In a small bowl, mix together the confectioners' sugar and lemon juice. Beat in the corn syrup, starting with 6 teaspoons and adding more if it is too thick, but use it thick if outlining and piping details on the cookies.

Separate the icing into small bowls and tint with food coloring to the desired shades.

When the cookies are completely cool, spread or pipe the icing on the cookies and allow the icing to set.

Snickerdoodles

There is just something about snickerdoodles that make the world seem like a better place. They're homey and innocent, unadorned but not plain, and just the right thing for an afternoon break with a glass of cold milk or a cup of hot tea.

No cookie jar should be without snickerdoodles!

16 tablespoons (2 sticks) unsalted butter, at room temperature

1½ cups plus 2 tablespoons sugar

2 large eggs, at room temperature

1 teaspoon pure vanilla extract

2¾ cups sweet rice flour blend

2 teaspoons baking powder

½ teaspoon kosher or fine sea salt

2 teaspoons ground cinnamon

Preheat the oven to 350 degrees. Line baking sheets with either parchment paper or silicone baking mats.

In the bowl of an electric mixer fitted with the paddle attachment, cream the butter and 1½ cups of the sugar on medium speed until very light and fluffy, about 5 minutes. Turn the speed to low, and add the eggs, one at a time, mixing well until each egg is fully incorporated, and scraping down the sides of the bowl with a spatula after each addition. Add the vanilla and mix well.

In a separate large mixing bowl, whisk together the sweet rice flour blend, baking powder, and salt.

Turn the mixer on low speed, and add the flour mixture to the butter mixture. Mix until just combined. Remove the bowl from mixer and scrape down the sides and bottom of the bowl well with a large spatula, making sure all ingredients are well mixed.

Mix the ground cinnamon with the remaining 2 tablespoons of sugar.

Form about 2 scant tablespoons of dough into a ball and roll in the cinnamon sugar, coating well. Repeat with the remaining dough.

Place the balls on the prepared baking sheets, about 3 inches apart. These

**Makes about
18 cookies**

cookies spread out quite a bit during baking so leave plenty of space on your baking sheets.

Bake the cookies for 12 to 15 minutes, rotating the baking sheets halfway through the baking time, until the edges of the cookies are golden brown. Let cool on the baking sheets for 5 minutes, then, using a spatula, transfer to a wire rack to cool completely.

Emma's Polish Cookies

My mother-in-law Emma was a tiny Polish woman with a huge heart. Every birthday or holiday was accompanied with big tins filled with her special homemade cookies.

I was so happy to be able to re-create her special cookies gluten-free, and continue the tradition with my husband and sons.

1 cup pecan halves

16 tablespoons (2 sticks) unsalted butter, at room temperature

2 cups sifted confectioners' sugar

1 teaspoon pure vanilla extract

$\frac{1}{2}$ teaspoon pure almond extract

2 cups sweet rice flour blend

$\frac{1}{4}$ teaspoon kosher or fine sea salt

Preheat the oven to 350 degrees. Line baking sheets with parchment paper or silicone baking mats.

Spread the pecan halves on a baking sheet and toast for about 10 to 12 minutes, or until they are hot and fragrant. Let cool and then chop coarsely. Leave the oven on.

In the bowl of an electric mixer fitted with the paddle attachment, cream the butter and 1 cup of the confectioners' sugar on medium speed until very light and fluffy, about 5 minutes. Add the vanilla and almond extracts and mix well.

In a separate large mixing bowl, whisk together the sweet rice flour blend and salt. Turn the speed to low, and gradually add the flour mixture to the butter mixture. Add the chopped pecans and mix just until the dough comes together. Roll tablespoonfuls of dough into balls and place on the prepared baking sheets, about 1 inch apart.

Bake the cookies for 20 to 25 minutes, rotating the baking sheets halfway through the baking time, until the cookies are lightly browned around the edges. Let cool on the baking sheets just until cool enough to handle.

**Makes about
24 cookies**

Put the remaining cup of confectioners' sugar in a medium bowl and toss the slightly cooled cookies in the sugar to coat. It is best to do this one cookie at a time. Place the cookies on a wire rack to finish cooling. Sift any remaining confectioners' sugar over the cooled cookies, if desired.

Chocolate Cherry Fudge Drops

Use the best quality dark chocolate you can find for these tender, fudgy cookies. Packed with dried cherries, chocolate chips, and chopped walnuts these cookies will satisfy anyone's sweet tooth.

Makes about 36 cookies depending on size

8 ounces bittersweet chocolate, chopped

2 tablespoons unsalted butter

2 large eggs

²/₃ cup sugar

¹/₄ cup sweet rice flour blend

1 teaspoon pure vanilla extract

¹/₄ teaspoon baking powder

³/₄ cup semisweet chocolate chips

1 cup dried cherries, roughly chopped

¹/₂ cup almonds, roughly chopped

Preheat the oven to 350 degrees. Line baking sheets with parchment paper or silicone baking mats.

Place the bittersweet chocolate and butter in a microwave-safe bowl and microwave on high for 2 to 3 minutes or until melted, stirring every 20 seconds. Or melt the chocolate and butter in a heatproof bowl set over a saucepan of barely simmering water, stirring occasionally; the bottom of the bowl should not touch the water. Let chocolate cool for a minute, then stir in the eggs, sugar, sweet rice flour blend, vanilla, and baking powder with a wooden spoon, stirring until everything is well combined. Stir in the chocolate chips, cherries, and nuts.

Using a rounded teaspoon or a small, 1-tablespoon ice cream scoop drop the dough in mounds onto the prepared baking sheets.

Bake the cookies for 8 to 10 minutes, or until the edges are firm and the tops are dull and cracked. Let cool on the baking sheets for 5 minutes, then transfer to a wire rack to finish cooling.

Oatmeal Raisin Cookies

Now that we can buy certified gluten-free oats, there is no reason not to indulge in this old-fashioned family favorite!

I like to make these cookies big, that way they get a tad crispy around the edges and are soft and chewy in the center.

16 tablespoons (2 sticks) unsalted butter, at room temperature

1 cup granulated sugar

1 cup firmly packed light brown sugar

2 large eggs, at room temperature

1 teaspoon pure vanilla extract

$2\frac{1}{2}$ cups gluten-free oats

2 cups sweet rice flour blend

$\frac{1}{2}$ teaspoon kosher or fine sea salt

1 teaspoon baking powder

1 teaspoon baking soda

$1\frac{1}{2}$ cups raisins

Preheat the oven to 375 degrees. Line baking sheets with either parchment paper or silicone baking mats.

In the bowl of an electric mixer fitted with the paddle attachment, cream the butter, granulated sugar, and brown sugar on medium speed until very light and fluffy, about 5 minutes. Turn the speed to low, and add the eggs, one at a time, mixing until each egg is fully incorporated, scraping down the sides of the bowl with a spatula after each addition. Add the vanilla and mix well.

Put 1½ cups of the oats in a blender or food processor and grind it to a powder. In a large mixing bowl, whisk together the ground oats, the remaining 1 cup of unground oats, sweet rice flour blend, salt, baking powder, and baking soda.

With the mixer on low speed, gradually add all but ½ cup of the flour-oat mixture to the butter mixture and mix until just combined. With a large spatula, scrape down the sides and bottom of the mixing bowl and make sure everything is well combined. Toss the raisins in with the remaining ½ cup flour-oat mixture and coat the raisins well. Fold into the batter.

Spoon the batter onto the prepared baking sheets, using between 1 and 2 tablespoons of batter per cookie, depending on how large you like them, leaving about 2 inches of space between each cookie.

Bake the cookies for 8 to 12 minutes. Let cool on the baking sheets for 5 minutes, then transfer to wire racks to finish cooling.

Makes 24 to 48 cookies depending on size

White Chocolate Macadamia Cookies

There is no way to feel deprived when eating these cookies! Better, in my opinion, than the packaged, gluten-filled variety you buy at the store. Packed with macadamia nuts and white chocolate chips, these are sure to be a favorite with your family and friends.

The surprise ingredient? Some milk chocolate grated into the batter. People won't realize what it is that gives these cookies that extra-special something.

16 tablespoons (2 sticks) unsalted butter, at room temperature

1 cup granulated sugar

1 cup firmly packed light brown sugar

2 large eggs, at room temperature

1 teaspoon pure vanilla extract

2½ cups gluten-free oats

2 cups sweet rice flour blend

½ teaspoon kosher or fine sea salt

1 teaspoon baking powder

1 teaspoon baking soda

4 ounces milk chocolate, grated

12 ounces white chocolate chips

12 ounces roasted, salted macadamia nuts (I prefer to leave the nuts whole but you can roughly chop, if desired)

Preheat the oven to 375 degrees. Line baking sheets with either parchment paper or silicone baking mats.

In the bowl of an electric mixer fitted with the paddle attachment, cream the butter, granulated sugar, and brown sugar on medium speed until very light and fluffy, about 5 minutes. Turn the speed to low, and add the eggs, one at a time, mixing well until each egg is fully incorporated, scraping down the sides of the bowl with a spatula after each addition. Add the vanilla and mix well.

Put the oats in a blender or food processor and grind it to a powder. In a large mixing bowl, whisk together the ground oats, sweet rice flour blend, salt, baking powder, and baking soda.

With the mixer on low speed, add the flour-oat mixture to the butter mixture gradually and mix until just combined. Add the grated milk chocolate. With a large spatula, scrape down the sides and bottom of the mixing bowl and make sure everything is well combined. Fold in the white chocolate chips and the macadamia nuts.

Spoon the batter onto the prepared baking sheets, using between 1 and 2 tablespoons of batter per cookie, depending on how large you like them, leaving about 2 inches of space between each cookie.

Bake the cookies for 8 to 12 minutes. Let cool on the baking sheets for 5 minutes and then transfer to wire racks with a spatula to finish cooling.

Makes 24 to 48 cookies depending on size

Almond Butter Chocolate Sandwiches

• Grain-free

My gorgeous nephew Kelton was the inspiration for these cookies as he has a decided sweet tooth and nasty peanut allergy. When creating this recipe, I was testing to see if my peanut butter cookie recipe would work equally well with almond butter—it does! And then I thought, "Hmmm, how about sandwiching in some chocolate ganache?" The combination is a winner!

The almond butter and bittersweet chocolate give these cookies a sophisticated flair. Substitute peanut butter and semisweet chocolate for a sweeter, more kid-friendly taste.

COOKIES

2 cups creamy almond butter

2 cups granulated sugar plus
   more for rolling the cookies

2 large eggs, lightly beaten with
   a fork

2 teaspoons baking powder

2 teaspoons pure vanilla extract

FILLING

8 ounces bittersweet chocolate
   chips

1 cup heavy whipping cream

Preheat the oven to 350 degrees. Line baking sheets with either parchment paper or silicone baking mats.

Stir the almond butter well to make sure the oil is well blended.

In a large bowl, using a wooden spoon, mix the almond butter with the 2 cups of sugar. Stir until well blended. Add the eggs, baking powder, and vanilla and mix well. Pour some additional sugar in a small bowl. Scoop out 1 tablespoon of the dough and roll it into a ball. Roll the dough ball in the sugar and place on the prepared baking sheets. Repeat with the remaining dough, spacing the balls about 1½ inches apart.

Dip a flat-bottomed glass or measuring cup in the sugar and press down gently on the balls to flatten them.

Bake the cookies for about 10 minutes. They should look puffed and cracked but not dry. Let cool 5 minutes on the baking sheets, then, using a spatula, transfer to wire racks to cool completely.

While cookies are baking, make the filling. Place the chocolate chips in a small, heatproof bowl. In a small saucepan, heat the cream over medium heat until it just comes to a boil. Pour the cream over the chocolate and let stand for 5 minutes, then whisk the cream and chocolate together until the mixture is shiny and smooth. Set aside until cooled and thickened, about 30 minutes. Whisk again before using.

To assemble the sandwiches, spread about 1½ teaspoons of the chocolate filling on the flat side of half the cookies. Top with the remaining cookies, flat side down, gently pressing the cookies together so that the filling spreads almost to the edge. Place on a wire rack for about 20 minutes more to let the filling firm up.

Makes 24 sandwich cookies

Pecan Tassies

For years I made these adorable little tart-like cookies at Christmas. I was so pleased when I was able to convert them to gluten-free.

One year when I was baking a lot of these, I went to the hardware store and asked them to cut a 1-inch diameter wooden dowel into a 4-inch length for me to use for forming the cookie. It cost me about 30 cents and I have had it for over twenty years. You can just as easily use the end of a French rolling pin (the kind that has no rollers or handles) or your fingers.

COOKIE CRUST	FILLING
8 tablespoons (1 stick) unsalted butter, at room temperature	1 large egg
	$^3/_4$ cup firmly packed light brown sugar
3 ounces cream cheese, at room temperature	1 tablespoon unsalted butter, at room temperature
1 cup sweet rice flour blend plus more for shaping the dough	1 teaspoon pure vanilla extract
	$^1/_8$ teaspoon kosher or fine sea salt
	$^1/_2$ cup chopped pecans

Using a food processor or an electric mixer fitted with the paddle attachment on medium speed, mix together the butter and cream cheese. Add the sweet rice flour blend and mix well. If using a mixer, make sure you scrape down the sides and bottom of the bowl with a large spatula to make sure the ingredients are well combined.

Shape the dough into 36 balls, using about 1 tablespoon of dough for each ball. Put the dough balls into ungreased, nonstick mini muffin cups, cover with plastic wrap, and refrigerate for 30 minutes. Alternatively you can place the balls into a plastic storage bag and refrigerate, and then put the chilled balls into the mini muffin cups when you are ready to bake them.

Preheat the oven to 325 degrees.

Makes about
36 tassies

With floured fingers, the flat end of a French rolling pin, or a piece of 1-inch dowel, gently press down on the dough, flattening it along the bottom and up the sides of the muffin cups. Be careful not to press the dough too much, which will make it too thin. If the dough warms up too much it is harder to press. Work quickly or rechill dough if it gets too soft.

Prepare the filling. Whisk together the egg, brown sugar, butter, vanilla, and salt until there are no lumps and the mixture is well blended.

Using a small spoon, fill each cookie crust with the mixture. Top each tassie with some chopped pecans.

Bake the tassies for approximately 25 minutes, or until the dough is browned and the filling is set. Let cool in the pans for 5 minutes, then transfer to a wire rack to cool completely.

Almond Raspberry Tassies

- Grain-free
- Dairy-free

Makes about
36 tassies

Crispy, sugar-coated, little flourless crusts filled with raspberry jam, these cookies may look humble but the taste is anything but.

These make a great snack for after school or to perk up the afternoon with a glass of milk or a cup of tea.

COOKIE CRUST

1 cup creamy almond butter

1 cup sugar plus more for rolling
   the cookies

1 large egg, lightly beaten with a
   fork

1 teaspoon baking powder

1 teaspoon vanilla extract

FILLING

1 cup good-quality raspberry jam

Preheat the oven to 350 degrees. Lightly spray mini muffin cups with gluten-free, nonstick cooking spray.

In a large bowl, using a wooden spoon, mix the almond butter with the sugar. Stir until well blended. Add the egg, baking powder, and vanilla and stir well. Pour some additional sugar in a small bowl. Scoop out 1 tablespoon of the dough and roll it into a ball. Roll the dough ball in the sugar and place in a prepared muffin cup. Repeat with the remaining dough.

With your fingers, the flat end of a French rolling pin, or a piece of 1-inch dowel dipped in sugar, gently press down on the dough, flattening it along the bottom and up the sides of the muffin cups. Be careful not to press the dough too much, which will make it too thin.

Bake the cookie crusts for approximately 10 to 15 minutes, or until the dough is browned and firm. Let cool in the pans for 5 minutes, then transfer to a wire rack to cool completely.

Fill each cookie with spoonfuls of raspberry jam.

Jam Thumbprint Cookies

With a shortbread-like cookie crust and raspberry filling, these little jewels make an excellent teatime treat.

Makes about 48 cookies

The dough is a little tricky to work with, but if you proceed slowly and with patience you will be rewarded. Feel free to substitute any type of jam you prefer.

16 tablespoons (2 sticks) unsalted butter, at room temperature	1/2 teaspoon kosher or fine sea salt
1 cup unsifted confectioners' sugar	2 teaspoons pure vanilla extract
	2 1/2 cups sweet rice flour blend
	1/2 cup good-quality raspberry jam

Preheat the oven to 350 degrees. Line baking sheets with parchment paper or silicone baking mats.

In the bowl of an electric mixer fitted with the paddle attachment, beat together the butter, sugar, salt, and vanilla on medium-high speed until smooth, about 2 minutes. Turn the speed to low, add the sweet rice flour blend and mix well, scraping down the sides and bottom of the mixing bowl with a large spatula to make sure all the ingredients are well combined.

Form balls out of the dough, using about 2 teaspoons of dough per ball (or use a small, 1-tablespoon ice cream scoop). Place the balls on the prepared baking sheets about 1 inch apart.

Bake the cookies for 8 minutes. Remove from the oven but leave the oven on. Let the cookies cool on the baking sheets for 1 to 2 minutes, then press your thumb into each one making a deep, wide indentation. You may have to cup your other hand around the outside of the cookie to stabilize it while making the indentation. Return the cookies to the oven and bake for another 9 to 11 minutes, or until the cookies are very lightly brown on the edges. Let cool on the baking sheets for 5 minutes, then transfer to a wire rack to cool completely.

Once the cookies are cool, spoon about 1/2 teaspoon of jam into each indentation.

Carrot Cake Cookies

My mother used to tell me that eating carrots was good for the eyesight. If she had made these cookies, I would have gladly eaten my carrots!

When a big slice of carrot cake is just too much, these cookies do the trick—all the goodness of carrot cake that fits in the palm of your hand.

COOKIES

16 tablespoons (2 sticks) unsalted butter, at room temperature

1 cup firmly packed light brown sugar

1 cup granulated sugar

2 large eggs, at room temperature

1 teaspoon pure vanilla extract

2 tablespoons freshly squeezed orange juice

1 tablespoon finely grated orange zest

2 cups sweet rice flour blend

1 teaspoon baking powder

1 teaspoon baking soda

1 teaspoon ground cinnamon

½ teaspoon kosher or fine sea salt

2 cups gluten-free oats

3 large carrots, finely grated (about 1½ cups)

1 cup raisins

FILLING

8 ounces cream cheese, at room temperature

8 tablespoons (1 stick) unsalted butter, at room temperature

¼ teaspoon kosher or fine sea salt

1 teaspoon pure vanilla extract

1 cup confectioners' sugar

Line baking sheets with parchment paper or silicone baking mats.

In the bowl of an electric mixer fitted with the paddle attachment, beat together the butter, brown sugar, and granulated sugar on medium speed. Add the eggs, one at a time, mixing well until each egg is fully incorporated, scraping down the sides of the bowl with a spatula after each addition. Add the vanilla, orange juice, and orange zest, and mix well.

Makes about
36 cookies

In a separate large mixing bowl, whisk together the sweet rice flour blend, baking powder, baking soda, cinnamon, and salt.

With the mixer on low speed, add half the flour mixture to the butter mixture. Add the oats, carrots, and raisins to the remaining flour mixture and toss well to coat. Add to the batter and mix well with a large spatula, making sure to scrape down the sides and bottom of the bowl well. Chill the dough in the refrigerator until firm, about 1 hour.

Preheat the oven to 350 degrees. Shape 1 tablespoon of the dough into a ball and place on the prepared baking sheets. Repeat with the remaining dough, spacing the balls about 2 inches apart. Gently flatten each dough ball.

Bake the cookies for 12 to 15 minutes rotating the baking sheets halfway through the baking time, until the cookies are crisp and browned. Let cool on the baking sheets for 5 minutes, then, using a spatula, transfer to a wire rack to cool completely.

While the cookies are baking, make the filling. In the bowl of an electric mixer fitted with the paddle attachment, blend together the cream cheese, butter, salt, and vanilla on medium speed. Turn off the mixer. Sift in the confectioners' sugar, then mix on low speed until smooth.

Put filling in the refrigerator to firm up while cookies finish baking and cooling.

To assemble the cookies, spread about 2 teaspoons of filling on the flat side of half the cookies. Top with the remaining cookies, placing them flat side down on the filling. Gently press the cookies together so that the filling spreads almost to the edge.

Red Velvet Whoopie Pies

Supposedly whoopie pies get their name from the fact that Amish women would occasionally pack these treats in the farmer's lunch boxes and when discovered the men would yell "Whoopie!"

Traditionally whoopie pies are two round mounds of chocolate cake with a creamy frosting sandwiched in between. For a twist on tradition, I love to make Red Velvet Whoopie pies.

COOKIE

- 8 tablespoons (1 stick) unsalted butter, at room temperature
- 1 cup granulated sugar
- 1 large egg, at room temperature
- 1 teaspoon pure vanilla extract
- 1 ounce red food coloring (about 2 tablespoons)
- 2 cups sweet rice flour blend
- 2 tablespoons unsweetened cocoa powder
- ½ teaspoon kosher or fine sea salt
- ½ cup buttermilk
- ½ teaspoon apple cider vinegar
- ½ teaspoon baking soda

FILLING

- 6 ounces cream cheese, at room temperature
- 3 tablespoons unsalted butter, at room temperature
- Pinch of kosher or fine sea salt
- 1 teaspoon pure vanilla extract
- 3 cups confectioners' sugar

Preheat the oven to 375 degrees. Line baking sheets with parchment paper or silicone baking mats.

In the bowl of an electric mixer fitted with the paddle attachment, cream the butter and sugar together until light and fluffy, about 3 minutes. Add the egg and mix well, scraping down the sides of the bowl with a large spatula. Add the vanilla and food coloring and mix well.

In a separate large mixing bowl, whisk together the sweet rice flour blend, cocoa powder, and salt. With the mixer on low, add half the flour blend mixture, then the buttermilk, and finally the rest of the flour blend mixture to the butter mixture and mix well.

In a small bowl mix the vinegar and baking soda together and then stir into the batter. Using a large spatula, scrape down the bottom and sides of the mixing bowl and make sure all the ingredients are incorporated. Drop the batter onto the prepared baking sheets using a small ice cream scoop or large tablespoon.

Bake the cookies for 7 to 9 minutes, or until the edges are set and the cookies are firm but springy to the touch. Let cool on the baking sheets for 5 minutes, then transfer to a wire rack to cool completely. While the cookies are cooling, make the filling.

In the bowl of an electric mixer fitted with the paddle attachment on medium speed, cream together the cream cheese, butter, salt, and vanilla until smooth. Turn the mixer off. Sift in the confectioners' sugar and starting with the mixer on low speed and slowly increasing the speed to medium, mix well.

With your hand, brush the crumbs off the bottom (flat side) of a cookie, spread with a generous amount of filling, then top with another cookie, flat side down on the filling. Repeat with remaining cookies and filling.

The cookies should be stored in the refrigerator but are best eaten unchilled, so take them out of the refrigerator 10 to 15 minutes prior to serving.

Makes about 1½ dozen depending on size

Pink Marshmallows

• Dairy-free

Every year at Christmas I make batches and batches of marshmallows and give them away as gifts along with some really good-quality hot chocolate mix. It's a delightful, homemade, thoughtful gift and what I hear most often is "I didn't know you could make marshmallows!"

I love the way the light pink looks on the dark brown of hot chocolate, but if you prefer your marshmallows more traditional then by all means leave out the food coloring and make yours white (or tint them any other color your heart desires).

Grapeseed oil, for brushing

3 cups granulated sugar

1¼ cups light corn syrup

¼ teaspoon salt

1½ cups water

4 envelopes unflavored gelatin

2 teaspoons pure vanilla extract

10 to 20 drops red food coloring

1 to 2 cups confectioners' sugar

Brush a 12 × 9-inch glass baking dish lightly with oil. Line with parchment paper, allowing a 2-inch overhang on the long sides. Brush the parchment paper with oil.

Put the granulated sugar, corn syrup, salt, and ¾ cup of the water into a medium saucepan. Bring to a boil over high heat, stirring to dissolve sugar. Once the mixture comes to a boil, continue to cook without stirring until the mixture registers between 238 and 245 degrees on a candy thermometer, about 10 minutes.

While the sugar mixture is cooking, dissolve the gelatin in the remaining ¾ cup of water in the bowl of an electric mixer fitted with the whisk attachment (or you can use beaters); let stand at least 5 minutes.

When the sugar mixture comes to the correct temperature, turn the mixer on low speed and very carefully add it to the gelatin mixture. Increase the speed to high and whip the mixture for 15 minutes, or until very thick and stiff. Add the vanilla and mix well. Add the food coloring, starting with a few drops, mixing and adding more until it reaches the desired color.

Pour the mixture into the prepared dish and smooth the top with a large spatula. Let stand, uncovered, at room temperature overnight.

The next day, sift about a cup of confectioners' sugar onto a work surface, unmold the marshmallow mixture onto the work surface, and remove the parchment paper. Sift some more confectioners' sugar on top. Oil a long sharp knife and cut the mixture into approximately 2-inch squares. (You may have to rinse the knife in hot water and re-oil occasionally as this mixture is very sticky.) Sift more confectioners' sugar over the cut marshmallows and roll them around in the sugar to make sure all the sides are coated.

Makes about 24 marshmallows

Candied Citrus Peels and Slices

* Grain-free
* Dairy-free

Candied citrus peels and slices are a way to give your desserts a pretty finishing touch. They also make great gifts, packed into decorative jars or bags. As an added bonus, the syrup left over from making them can be poured into a bottle and kept on hand to stir into cocktails, sweeten iced tea, or brush onto muffins and cakes.

You can make more than one type of citrus at a time, but I always do peels separate from slices as the slices need to be cooked for about 10 minutes longer than the peels. You can also double or triple this recipe; something I often do as my family loves to munch on these little gems as a sweet-tart snack.

These can be made at least a week ahead and stored in an airtight container or a Ziploc bag.

Other recipes for candied citrus call for preboiling the zest three times in a clean change of water each time before boiling them in the syrup. I tested this recipe many times over and found that step unnecessary.

CANDIED CITRUS PEELS	CANDIED CITRUS SLICES
2 large oranges or 4 lemons or limes, preferably organic, washed well	2 large oranges or 4 lemons or limes, preferably organic, washed well
3 cups granulated sugar	3 cups granulated sugar
2 cups water	2 cups water

To prepare candied citrus peels, remove the peel from the washed oranges, lemons, or limes with a vegetable peeler in strips, trying to remove only the colored part of the zest and not the bitter white pith. If there is white pith on the zest scrape it off with a sharp knife.

Bring 2 cups of the sugar and the water to a boil in a large, heavy saucepan. Once it starts to boil, add the zest, turn the heat down to medium-low, and let simmer for 30 to 35 minutes.

Makes approximately 1 cup

Pour the remaining cup of sugar into a bowl or onto a plate. Remove the citrus peels from the syrup and toss in the sugar to coat.

Lay the strips on a piece of parchment paper or on a wire rack and let air-dry for about 2 hours. Store in an airtight container.

To prepare candied citrus slices, cut the citrus into thin slices, about ¼ inch thick, and carefully remove any seeds.

Bring 2 cups of the sugar and the water to a boil in a large, heavy saucepan. Once it starts to boil, add the citrus slices, turn the heat down to medium-low, and let simmer for 45 minutes.

Pour the remaining cup of sugar into a bowl or onto a plate. Remove the citrus slices from the syrup and toss in the sugar to coat.

Lay the slices on a piece of parchment paper or on a wire rack and let air-dry for about 2 hours. Store in an airtight container.

Grain-free Magic Bars

• Grain-free

Makes 24 bars

Magic bars are one of the simplest cookies to make. Just layer ingredients into a pan, bake, cut, and serve.

The flavors in these grain-free bars are a little more grown-up than the normal with dark chocolate, dried cherries, and sliced almonds. Feel free to change this to suit your own tastes. Milk or bittersweet chocolate chips work equally well, and you can substitute whatever dried fruit and nuts you like.

BASE

1½ cups blanched almond flour

2 tablespoons sugar

¼ cup honey

3 tablespoons unsalted butter, melted

¼ teaspoon kosher or fine sea salt

TOPPINGS

2 cups semisweet chocolate chips

1 cup dried cherries, chopped

1 cup sliced almonds

One 14-ounce can sweetened condensed milk

1⅓ cups sweetened flaked coconut

Preheat the oven to 325 degrees. Spray a 12 × 9-inch baking dish with gluten-free, nonstick cooking spray.

To make the base, combine the almond flour, sugar, honey, melted butter, and salt. Press evenly into the bottom of the prepared baking dish.

Layer the almond flour base evenly with chocolate chips, dried cherries, and sliced almonds. Pour the sweetened condensed milk evenly over the whole thing. Top with the coconut, and press down firmly with a spatula or fork.

Bake the bars 30 to 40 minutes, or until lightly browned. Cool; I find the bars easier to cut if they have been refrigerated for about an hour. Cut into 3 × 3-inch squares and then cut the squares in half to form triangles.

Lemon Squares

I love lemon desserts but ironically I usually find they are made too sweet thus masking the lemon flavor. These lemon squares are bursting with lemon flavor and have, in my opinion, the perfect balance between sweet and tart.

CRUST

16 tablespoons (2 sticks) unsalted butter, at room temperature

½ cup granulated sugar

2 cups sweet rice flour blend

¼ teaspoon kosher or fine sea salt

Pinch of kosher or fine sea salt

2 tablespoons finely grated lemon zest (4 to 6 lemons)

1 cup freshly squeezed lemon juice

1 cup sweet rice flour blend

Confectioners' sugar for dusting

FILLING

7 large eggs

2 cups granulated sugar

Lightly spray a 12 × 9-inch glass baking dish with gluten-free, nonstick cooking spray.

In the bowl of an electric mixer fitted with the paddle attachment, cream the butter and sugar on medium speed until very light and fluffy, about 3 minutes.

In a separate large mixing bowl, whisk together the sweet rice flour blend and salt. With the mixer on low speed, add the flour mixture to the butter mixture and mix until just blended. Dump the dough into the prepared baking dish and press it out with your hands, building up a ½-inch edge on all sides. Chill the dough in refrigerator for 30 minutes.

Preheat the oven to 350 degrees.

Bake the crust for 15 to 20 minutes, or until very lightly browned. Set aside to cool. Leave the oven on.

Prepare the filling. Whisk the eggs, sugar, salt, lemon zest, and lemon juice

Makes about
12 squares or
24 triangles

together. Slowly whisk in the sweet rice flour a little at a time. Pour over the cooled crust and bake for 30 to 35 minutes, or until the filling is set. Let cool to room temperature.

Cut into 3-inch squares, or you can cut the squares into triangles. Dust with confectioners' sugar.

Salted Peanut Caramel Brownies

The moist, fudgy yet cake-like base of these brownies is terrific on its own but with the addition of a layer of rich caramel and topped with salty peanuts the simple brownie is transformed into something so sublime, so sinfully delectable, so seriously addictive you may never be satisfied with a plain old brownie again.

The brownies will be easier to cut if you let them come to room temperature after refrigerating. As the caramel softens the brownies taste better and better.

BROWNIES

1 cup sweet rice flour blend

$\frac{1}{2}$ teaspoon kosher or fine sea salt

1 teaspoon baking powder

12 ounces bittersweet chocolate chips (about 1 bag)

16 tablespoons (2 sticks) unsalted butter

1 cup sugar

3 large eggs, lightly beaten

$1\frac{1}{2}$ teaspoons instant espresso powder

1 teaspoon pure vanilla extract

CARAMEL NUT TOPPING

1 cup heavy whipping cream

6 tablespoons ($\frac{3}{4}$ stick) unsalted butter

1 teaspoon kosher or fine sea salt

$1\frac{1}{2}$ cups sugar

$\frac{1}{4}$ cup light corn syrup

$\frac{1}{4}$ cup water

$1\frac{1}{2}$ cups salted dry-roasted peanuts, chopped

Preheat the oven to 350 degrees. Lightly spray a 12 × 9-inch baking dish with gluten-free, nonstick cooking spray.

In a medium mixing bowl, whisk together the sweet rice flour blend, salt, and baking powder.

In a large microwave-safe bowl, melt the chocolate chips and butter together in the microwave for about 3½ minutes, or until the butter is fully melted and the chocolate is mostly melted, stirring every 20 seconds. Or melt

the chocolate in a heatproof bowl set over a saucepan of barely simmering water; the bottom of the bowl should not touch the water. Stir until the chocolate is fully melted, and the mixture is combined and glossy. Stir in the sugar, then the eggs, flour mixture, instant espresso powder, and vanilla. Pour the batter into the prepared baking dish and bake for 30 minutes, or until a toothpick inserted in the center comes out clean. Do not overbake!

While the brownies are baking prepare the caramel. Heat the cream, butter, and salt in a saucepan, stirring occasionally, until the cream is hot and the butter is fully melted. Remove from the heat.

In a large, straight-sided saucepan, combine the sugar, corn syrup, and water and cook over medium heat until the mixture turns an amber color (like a new copper penny), about 6 minutes. Do not stir the mixture while it cooks; gently swirl the pan only as often as necessary to melt the sugar and make sure the mixture colors evenly. Take the pan off the heat and carefully pour in the warm cream mixture while whisking. The mixture may splatter as you add the cream so be careful not to burn yourself. Return the pan to the heat and cook gently for 5 minutes, stirring. Let the mixture cool a little.

When the brownies are done, let them cool for 10 to 15 minutes (you want them warm to the touch but not hot), then pour the warm caramel over the top. Top evenly with the chopped peanuts and refrigerate for about an hour to set the layers (this can be made a day ahead, covered with plastic wrap, and kept refrigerated). Remove the brownies from the refrigerator and let set at room temperature for about half an hour; this will make cutting easier. Cut into twelve 3-inch squares with a sharp knife. If you want bite-size brownies, it is easiest to cut large squares, remove them from the pan with a spatula, and then cut into quarters on a cutting board.

Black Bean Brownies

Yes, you read that correctly—these brownies are made with canned black beans. Talk about sneaking healthy stuff into your food!

I won't kid you, these brownies don't taste exactly the same as the brownies you may be used to but they are deliciously rich and fudgy. Besides having no grains, dairy, or refined sugar they are low in fat.

I find these brownies taste even better the next day.

- Grain-free
- Sugar-free
- Dairy-free

Makes about
16 brownies

One 15.5-ounce can unsalted black beans, rinsed and drained
3 large eggs
3 tablespoons grapeseed oil
1/4 cup unsweetened cocoa powder

Pinch of kosher or fine sea salt
1 teaspoon pure vanilla extract
3/4 cup agave nectar
1 teaspoon instant espresso powder
1/2 cup chopped walnuts

Preheat the oven to 350 degrees. Lightly spray an 8 × 8-inch square baking dish with gluten-free, nonstick cooking spray.

Combine the drained black beans, eggs, grapeseed oil, cocoa powder, salt, vanilla, agave nectar, and espresso powder in a blender and blend until smooth. Add the walnuts and give the blender a very quick whirl just to combine the nuts. Pour the batter into the prepared baking dish. Bake the brownies for about 30 minutes, or until the top is dry and the edges start to pull away from the sides of the dish. Let cool in the pan and then cut into small squares.

Pies, Tarts, and Such

Perfect Pie Crust

I believe that the crust of a pie should be as tasty as the filling so I prefer an all butter pie crust. If you cannot have dairy, then substitute solid all vegetable shortening for the butter.

Most people think the purpose for resting the pie crust in the refrigerator before rolling is to let the gluten settle, which would make no sense with gluten-free pie crust. The real purpose is for the moisture to become evenly distributed throughout the dough. So don't skip this step.

This recipe is for sweet pies. If using the dough for a savory dish such as quiche, cut the sugar to 1 teaspoon.

For a unique variation, try the chocolate pie crust; it adds a surprising twist to pudding-type pie fillings or berry pies.

8 tablespoons (1 stick) unsalted butter	1¼ cups sweet rice flour blend plus more for rolling
2 to 4 tablespoons water	1 teaspoon kosher or fine sea salt
	2 tablespoons sugar

Cut the butter into ½-inch pieces and place in the freezer for 15 to 30 minutes.

Add some ice cubes to the water and let it get ice cold while preparing the dry ingredients.

Combine the sweet rice flour blend, salt, and sugar in the bowl of a food processor. Pulse 5 to 6 times to combine. Add the butter and pulse 6 to 8 times, or until the mixture resembles coarse meal with some pea-size pieces of butter.

With the processor running, add ice water, 1 tablespoon at a time, until the mixture just barely starts to clump together. If you pinch some of the crumbly dough together and it holds then you have enough water, if not add more a little at a time. You do not want to add any more water than is absolutely necessary.

Remove the dough from the machine and form into a disk. Wrap the disk in

plastic wrap and refrigerate for at least 1 hour, or for as long as 2 to 3 days. Since the dough is so crumbly and does not hold together at this point, I find it easier (and far less messy) to pour the mixture into a large food storage bag and form it into a disk using the bag to help. Then just close up the bag and put it in the refrigerator. Remove the dough from refrigerator 5 minutes before rolling.

To roll the dough, lay a piece of wax paper on a work surface and sprinkle with some sweet rice flour blend. Lay the chilled disk on the floured paper, sprinkle with some more flour, and lay another piece of wax paper on top. Roll the dough into a circle approximately 12 inches in diameter. Remove the top sheet of wax paper and carefully flip the dough into a 9-inch pie plate. Remove the other sheet of wax paper. Push the dough very gently down so it lines the bottom and sides of the pie plate. If the dough splits or breaks, just push it back together with your fingers. Trim the edge of the pie crust to about a ½- to ¾-inch overhang. Tuck the overhang under and pinch the edge of the dough into a decorative border.

If you do not have a food processor, then whisk the dry ingredients together, rub the butter into the dry ingredients with your fingertips, and add the water using a fork. Just be sure to work quickly as you do not want to melt the butter.

Sometimes a recipe will call for a prebaked or blind-baked pie crust; here's how to do that.

Freeze the pie crust in the pie plate for at least 30 minutes.

Preheat the oven to 350 degrees.

Place a piece of parchment paper (or aluminum foil) in the bottom and up the sides of the pie crust. Fill with dried beans, rice, or pie weights. (I prefer dried black beans as they help distribute the heat better and are much less expensive than pie weights. I use the same beans over and over.) Bake the crust for 20 minutes. Remove the weights and wax paper, poke a few holes in the bottom of the crust with a fork, and return to the oven for 10 minutes, or until golden brown. Let the pie crust cool completely before filling.

VARIATION

Chocolate Pie Crust: Add 1½ tablespoons cocoa powder to the dry ingredients and proceed as above. The dough may require just a tad more water. Make sure to brush off the excess sweet rice flour blend after rolling.

Makes one
9-inch pie
crust

Tart Shell

Makes one 11-inch or eight 4-inch tart shells

This is a basic tart shell recipe that can be baked and filled with any number of fillings.

The tart shells need to be weighted while baking. Place parchment paper or aluminum foil over the dough and fill with pie weights, rice, or dried beans. Depending on the recipe you are using, you can partially or fully bake the tart shells.

8 tablespoons (1 stick) unsalted butter, at room temperature

½ cup confectioners' sugar

2 large eggs

Pinch of kosher or fine sea salt

1¾ cups sweet rice flour blend plus more for dusting

In an electric mixer fitted with a paddle attachment, cream together the butter and confectioners' sugar on medium-high speed until light and fluffy, about 2 minutes. Add the eggs and salt and mix well. Turn the mixer on low speed, add the sweet rice flour blend, and mix until the dough just comes together. Gather the dough into a ball, flatten into a disk, and wrap in plastic wrap. Refrigerate for 1 hour.

Preheat the oven to 350 degrees.

Put a large piece of wax or parchment paper on a work surface and sprinkle lightly with some sweet rice flour blend. Put the dough on top of the flour and sprinkle with some more flour. Top with another sheet of paper. Roll out the dough between the two sheets of paper, until large enough to fill the tart pan or pans you are using. Cut the dough and transfer to the tart pan(s). If the dough tears while cutting or transferring, just pinch it back together. Line the dough with parchment paper and fill with dried beans, rice, or pie weights.

For a partially baked tart shell, bake shell for 15 minutes. For a fully baked tart shell, bake for 15 minutes, remove the parchment paper and weights, prick the shell all over with the tines of a fork, and return to oven for 20 to 25 minutes more, or until lightly browned. Allow the shell(s) to cool completely before filling.

Shortbread Tart Crust

A quick whirl in the food processor and no rolling makes this an easy crust for tarts. I love that this dough is just pressed into the tart shells. This rich, buttery crust is perfect when filled with pastry cream, pudding, or citrus curd.

Makes one 11-inch or six 4-inch tart shells

1¹⁄₂ cups sweet rice flour blend
¹⁄₃ cup confectioners' sugar
¹⁄₂ teaspoon kosher or fine sea salt

¹⁄₂ teaspoon pure vanilla extract
12 tablespoons (1¹⁄₂ sticks) cold, unsalted butter, cut into ¹⁄₂-inch pieces

Lightly spray removable bottom tart pan(s) with gluten-free, nonstick cooking spray.

Put the sweet rice flour blend, confectioners' sugar, and salt in a food processor. Pulse several times to combine. Add the vanilla and butter pieces and pulse until the dough just starts to come together and form clumps. The dough will still be very crumbly—gather some in your hand and squeeze it—it should hold its shape when you open your hand.

Press the dough into prepared pan(s) evenly on the bottom and up the sides. You can use the bottom of a measuring cup to help even out the bottom. Prick the bottom and sides of the dough all over with a fork to keep the dough from puffing too much while baking. Place the crust into the freezer for at least 15 minutes.

Preheat the oven to 350 degrees.

Bake the chilled tart crust for 15 to 20 minutes, or until the edges are firm and the crust is golden brown. Let the crust(s) cool completely in the tart pan(s) before filling.

The shortbread crust can be baked a day ahead. Wrap in plastic wrap and store at room temperature.

Chocolate Shortbread Tart Crust

Makes one
11-inch or six
4-inch tart
shells

Why should chocolate be reserved for the filling? This is a great alternative crust that is as easy to make as it is decadent. Chocolate lovers rejoice!

1 cup sweet rice flour blend

$^1/_3$ cup unsweetened cocoa
    powder

$^2/_3$ cup confectioners' sugar

$^1/_2$ teaspoon kosher or fine sea salt

$^1/_2$ teaspoon pure vanilla
    extract

12 tablespoons (1$^1/_2$ sticks) cold,
    unsalted butter, cut into
    $^1/_2$-inch pieces

Lightly spray one 11-inch or six 4-inch removable bottom tart pan(s) with gluten-free, nonstick cooking spray.

Put the sweet rice flour, cocoa powder, confectioners' sugar, and salt in a food processor. Pulse several times to combine. Add the vanilla and butter pieces and process just until the dough forms into a ball. The dough will be soft and a little sticky.

Press the dough into the prepared pan(s) firmly and evenly in the bottom and up the sides. You can use the bottom of a measuring cup to help even out the bottom. Prick the bottom and sides of the dough all over with a fork to keep the dough from puffing too much while baking. Place the crust into the freezer for at least 15 minutes.

Preheat the oven to 350 degrees.

Bake the chilled crust for 15 to 20 minutes or until the edges are firm but the center is still a little soft. The crust will firm as it cools. Let the crust cool completely before removing the outer ring of the tart pan(s).

The chocolate shortbread crust(s) can be baked a day ahead. Once cooled, wrap in plastic wrap and store at room temperature.

Nut Crust

~~~~~~~~~~~~~~~~~

This crust can be used for recipes typically calling for graham cracker crusts. Not only will the crust be gluten-free, but also the nuts will add a little protein to the dessert. Use any type of nuts you like. I find pecans and walnuts work especially well. Dry-roasted, salted peanuts make for a nice, salty twist especially if the filling is made with peanut butter.

    This is a great crust for no-bake cheesecakes or to fill with pudding or fruit. Bake the crust first even if you are filling it with something that needs to be baked, such as apple pie filling. Allow the crust to cool completely if you are filling it with a no-bake filling such as pudding.

• Grain-free

Makes one 9-inch pie crust

2 cups nuts

1 tablespoon granulated sugar

1 small pinch of kosher or fine sea salt

6 tablespoons (³/₄ stick) unsalted butter, melted

Spray a 9-inch pie plate with gluten-free, nonstick cooking spray. Preheat the oven to 350 degrees.

    Put nuts, sugar, and salt in a food processor and pulse until ground. Pulse in the melted butter. Press the mixture evenly into the prepared pie plate. Make sure you even it out. Bake 12 to 15 minutes, or until browned and fairly set. It may still be a little soft when it comes out of the oven; don't worry, it will firm up. Cool completely before filling especially if the filling is no-bake.

Meringue Pie Crust

- Grain-free
- Dairy-free

Makes one
9-inch pie
crust

This is the perfect crust for upside-down lemon meringue pie, but is also wonderful filled with pudding, fresh fruit, and whipped cream or pastry cream and berries.

2 large egg whites	½ cup granulated
¼ teaspoon cream of tartar	sugar
¼ teaspoon kosher or fine sea salt	½ teaspoon vanilla extract

Spray a 9-inch pie plate with gluten-free, nonstick cooking spray. Preheat the oven to 300 degrees.

In the bowl of an electric mixer fitted with a whisk attachment, beat the egg whites, cream of tartar, and salt starting on low speed gradually increasing to high speed until soft peaks form. Gradually add the sugar and continue to beat until the mixture is very stiff and glossy. To make sure the sugar is properly dissolved, rub a little of the mixture between your thumb and forefinger; it should be smooth and not gritty. If still gritty, continue to beat until smooth, which means the sugar has completely dissolved. Add the vanilla and mix in well.

Spoon the mixture into the prepared pan, and form a shell by spreading the mixture up the sides of the pie plate.

Bake the crust for 50 minutes. Turn off the oven and leave the crust in the oven for another hour. Remove the crust from the oven and allow it to cool completely.

A meringue crust is best used the day it is baked as humidity will soften it. It is also preferable to fill the crust just prior to serving.

Banana Cream Pie

When my good friend and fellow chef Darrell came to visit, we made numerous versions of banana cream pie until we found a recipe we loved. It was tough work tasting pie after pie but somehow we made it through! And my husband and the cable repairman were very willing guinea pigs.

CRUST

One 9-inch Perfect Pie Crust,
    prebaked (page 137)

FILLING

2 large eggs

3 tablespoons cornstarch

1 cup cold, whole milk

1 cup half-and-half

1/2 cup plus 2 tablespoons
    granulated sugar

Pinch of kosher or fine
    sea salt

1 tablespoon cold butter

1 teaspoon pure vanilla extract

4 medium bananas

TOPPING

1 cup heavy cream

2 teaspoons granulated sugar

1/2 teaspoon pure vanilla extract

Prepare and bake one 9-inch Perfect Pie Crust according to the recipe directions.

In a large bowl, whisk the eggs well.

In a small bowl, mix the cornstarch with about 1/2 cup of the cold milk.

In a large saucepan, mix the remaining milk, the half-and-half, the sugar, and the salt together. Heat over medium heat, stirring occasionally, until the mixture comes to a boil. Gradually pour about one-fourth of the hot mixture into the eggs and whisk well. Pour the whisked eggs into the saucepan along with the cornstarch mixture and bring to a boil over medium to medium-low heat, stirring constantly. Continue to boil gently for 1 minute, stirring constantly. Take the mixture off the heat and stir in the cold butter and vanilla. Put

Serves 6 to 8

a strainer or sieve over a bowl and push the pudding through to remove any lumps.

Peel the bananas and slice them diagonally in about ¼-inch slices. Reserve a few slices for the top as garnish. Layer the rest of the bananas on the bottom of the cooled, prebaked pie crust. Pour the pudding over the bananas and smooth the top with a spatula. Let the filling cool for about half an hour, then refrigerate until cold and firm, about 4 hours.

Whip the cream with the sugar and vanilla until stiff peaks form. Spread over the pie, garnish with reserved banana slices, and serve.

Mexican Chocolate Cake with
Cinnamon Whipped Cream, page 39

Pound Cake, page 23

Coconut Cupcakes, page 54

Peanut Butter–Filled Chocolate Cupcakes,
page 75

Black Forest Cupcakes, page 52

Lemon-Lime Cupcakes, page 58

Cornmeal Strawberry Shortcake,
page 127

Salted Peanut Caramel Brownies,
page 131

Grain-free Magic Bars, page 128

Lemon Squares, page 129

Red Velvet Whoopie Pies, page 122

Mascarpone Berry Pie, page 150

Chocolate Chunk Coconut Macaroons, page 94

Chocolate Cherry Fudge Drops, page 109

White Chocolate Macadamia Cookies, page 112

Lemon Sugar Cookies, page 103

Raspberry Tart, page 167

Blueberry Streusel Pie

Tapioca is a gluten-free starch with a clean flavor that holds up well to long cooking times, making it the ideal thickener for berry pies. Use minute tapioca or tapioca flour rather than regular tapioca or the grains will not dissolve properly. It is also important to combine the tapioca with the fruit and sugar and set aside for 15 minutes to get the desired result.

Without gluten, pie crusts don't stretch well and for that reason I prefer streusel toppings for pies rather than a top crust. The touch of lemon in this streusel accentuates the sweet, vibrant blueberries.

CRUST

1 recipe Perfect Pie Crust
   (page 137)

FILLING

2 pints fresh blueberries
²/₃ cup granulated sugar
¼ cup minute tapioca
Juice of 1 lemon
Zest of 1 lemon, finely grated
1 tablespoon unsalted butter, cut
   into very small pieces

STREUSEL TOPPING

½ cup sweet rice flour blend
¼ cup granulated sugar
Pinch of kosher or fine
   sea salt
Zest of 1 lemon, finely grated
3 tablespoons cold, unsalted
   butter, cut into small
   pieces
Juice of ½ lemon

Prepare the pie crust. Roll out the dough according to the recipe directions and place it in a 9-inch deep dish pie pan.

Preheat the oven to 400 degrees. Line a baking sheet with aluminum foil.

In a large mixing bowl, combine the blueberries, sugar, tapioca, lemon juice, and zest. Set aside for 15 minutes. Pour the blueberry mixture into the pie crust and dot with the pieces of butter. Place a piece of aluminum foil loosely over the pie and bake for 35 minutes.

Serves 8

Prepare the streusel topping. Whisk together the sweet rice flour, sugar, salt, and lemon zest in a medium mixing bowl. Cut the butter into the flour with a pastry cutter or your fingertips until it looks like coarse crumbs. Squeeze the lemon juice into the mixture and toss until crumbly.

Remove the foil from the pie, sprinkle the streusel topping over the top of the pie, and continue to bake, uncovered, for 15 to 20 minutes, or until the streusel is browned and the blueberries are bubbly. Let cool.

Dairy-free Pumpkin Pie

For my grandson Julian, Thanksgiving means one thing—pumpkin pie! Since he is intolerant to dairy, I needed to convert my traditional recipe to be not only gluten-free but dairy-free as well.

• Dairy-free

This recipe substitutes coconut milk for evaporated milk. By bumping up the cinnamon just a tad and adding vanilla extract there is no "coconutty" flavor to the pie.

To make this pie extra-special, top with nondairy whipped topping, or whipped coconut cream.

CRUST
One 9-inch dairy-free version of Perfect Pie Crust (page 137)

FILLING
2 large eggs

One 15-ounce can pure pumpkin puree (not pumpkin pie filling)

$1/2$ cup granulated sugar

$1/4$ cup firmly packed light brown sugar

$1\frac{1}{2}$ teaspoons ground cinnamon

$1/2$ teaspoon kosher or fine sea salt

$1/2$ teaspoon ground ginger

$1/4$ teaspoon ground cloves

2 teaspoons pure vanilla extract

One 13.5-ounce can coconut milk

Preheat the oven to 425 degrees.

Prepare a dairy-free version of the Perfect Pie Crust, substituting solid all vegetable shortening for the butter.

Roll out the dough according to the recipe directions and place in a 9-inch deep dish pie plate.

In a large bowl whisk the eggs. Whisk in the pumpkin, sugars, ground cinnamon, salt, ginger, cloves, and vanilla. Shake the can of coconut milk well and gradually whisk into the pumpkin mixture until well blended. Pour the mixture into the pie crust.

Serves 6 to 8

Bake the pie for 15 minutes. Reduce the oven temperature to 350 degrees, and continue to bake for 40 to 45 minutes, or until a knife inserted into the center comes out clean. Allow the pie to cool for at least 2 hours, then refrigerate until serving. This pie tastes better when refrigerated for a few hours.

Mascarpone Berry Pie

This is an elegant take on those no-bake cheesecake pies and is showstopping gorgeous! I like to use a combination of fresh berries. For an even bigger pop of color, substitute some of the berries with some cherries or diced mango or papaya.

Serves 8

CRUST
1 recipe Nut Crust (pecans go especially well with the filling) (page 143)

FILLING
8 ounces mascarpone cheese, at room temperature

¼ cup granulated sugar

1 tablespoon freshly squeezed lemon juice (about half a lemon)

1 teaspoon lemon zest (about half a lemon), finely grated

2 cups heavy whipping cream

1½ teaspoons pure vanilla extract

2 pints assorted fresh berries

¼ cup seedless raspberry jam

2 tablespoons berry-flavored liqueur such as Crème de Cassis or Chambord

Prepare the nut crust according to the recipe directions and allow it to cool completely.

In the bowl of an electric mixer fitted with the paddle attachment, beat the mascarpone cheese and sugar on medium speed until smooth. Add the lemon juice and zest and mix.

In a clean bowl of an electric mixer fitted with the whisk attachment, whip the cream with the vanilla on high speed until stiff peaks form. Take a big scoop of the whipped cream and stir it into the cheese mixture to lighten it, then gently fold in the rest. Spoon the filling into the cooled nut crust, cover lightly with plastic wrap, and refrigerate for at least 8 hours. This pie can be made 1 day ahead.

Just before serving, heap the berries on top of the pie, stir the jam and liqueur together, and drizzle over the fruit.

Pies, Tarts, and Such

Triple Coconut Pie

• Dairy-free

With flaked coconut in the filling and crust, coconut milk as a base for the filling, and toasted coconut topping, this pie is a coconut lover's delight.

CRUST AND TOPPING

1⅓ cups sweetened flaked coconut

1 cup sliced almonds

1 tablespoon granulated sugar

¼ teaspoon kosher or fine sea salt

1 tablespoon grapeseed (or other neutral-tasting vegetable oil)

FILLING

Two 13.5-ounce cans coconut milk

¼ cup cornstarch

¾ cup granulated sugar

¼ teaspoon kosher or fine sea salt

5 large egg yolks

1 cup sweetened flaked coconut

1½ teaspoons pure vanilla extract

½ teaspoon pure almond extract

Preheat the oven to 350 degrees. Lightly spray a 9-inch pie pan with gluten-free, nonstick cooking spray.

Spread ⅓ cup of the coconut on a baking sheet in an even layer.

Put the remaining 1 cup coconut, almonds, sugar, and salt in a food processor and pulse until the nuts and coconut are finely ground. Add the oil and pulse until it starts to come together. Pat the mixture into the prepared pie pan. Put the baking sheet with the flaked coconut and the pie crust into the oven and bake for 10 minutes. Check on the coconut flakes after about 8 minutes. You want them nicely browned and fragrant. Set aside the toasted coconut flakes.

Prepare the filling. Shake the cans of coconut milk well. Mix ½ cup of the coconut milk with the cornstarch. Set aside.

In a medium saucepan, combine the remaining coconut milk with the sugar and salt. Bring just to a boil over medium-high heat. Whisk the egg yolks well.

Simply . . . Gluten-free Desserts

Gradually pour about ½ cup of the heated coconut milk mixture into the yolks, whisking well. Pour the egg yolk mixture and cornstarch mixture into the heated coconut milk and bring the mixture back to a gentle boil, whisking constantly. Once the mixture starts to boil, cook for 1 to 2 minutes more. The mixture should thicken to the consistency of pudding. Do not cook longer than 2 minutes or the cornstarch will lose its potency. Remove from heat and stir in the sweetened flaked coconut and the extracts, combining well. Pour the filling into the completely cooled pie crust and cover the pie with plastic wrap, pressing the plastic wrap directly on the surface of the filling to prevent a skin from forming. Refrigerate until completely cold, about 2 hours.

Sprinkle the top of the pie with the reserved toasted coconut before serving.

Serves 6 to 8

Upside-Down Lemon Meringue Pie

One of the first foods I recall falling in love with was lemon meringue pie. Before I had mastered gluten-free pie crust, I began making my lemon meringue pies upside down—the meringue was the crust not the topping. It was a huge hit.

Make sure that you fill the meringue crust with the lemon filling just prior to serving so the crust does not get soggy.

CRUST
1 recipe Meringue Pie Crust
   (page 144)

FILLING
4 large egg yolks
1/3 cup cornstarch
1 1/2 cups water
1 1/3 cups granulated sugar
1/4 teaspoon kosher or fine sea salt
3 tablespoons cold, unsalted
   butter
1/2 cup freshly squeezed lemon
   juice
1 tablespoon finely grated lemon
   zest

TOPPING
1 cup heavy whipping cream
1 teaspoon sugar
Finely sliced lemon slices for
   garnish, optional

Prepare the Meringue Pie Crust according to the recipe directions.

Prepare the filling. Put the eggs in a medium bowl and whisk well.

In a medium saucepan, using a whisk, combine the cornstarch, water, sugar, and salt. Bring to a boil over medium heat, stirring frequently, and boil for 1 minute. Remove from the heat and add about one-fourth of the hot mixture to the egg yolks and whisk well. Add the rest of the mixture to the eggs gradually, whisking well. When all of the hot mixture is added to the egg yolks, pour the mixture back into the saucepan, turn the heat to low, and cook for 1 more minute, stirring constantly. The mixture should be thick. Take the mixture off the heat and gently stir in the cold butter, lemon juice, and lemon zest.

Put the mixture into a bowl and cover with plastic wrap, pressing the plastic wrap directly on the surface of the lemon mixture to prevent a skin from forming. Refrigerate until cold, about 2 hours.

Just prior to serving, whip the heavy cream with the sugar until stiff peaks form, but do not overmix. Pour the lemon mixture into the meringue pie crust. Top with whipped cream. Garnish with lemon slices, if desired, and serve immediately.

Peanut Butter Chocolate Pie

I can't make this pie without thinking of my dearest friend Angie. We once took a whole peanut butter pie, cut it right down the middle and then proceeded to each eat half of it. I can't remember if we were nursing a heartbreak, celebrating some triumph, or if it was just Sunday, but I remember the pie!

This is, hands down, my favorite dessert to make when asked to bring a dish to someone else's party or when I'm entertaining. The reasons? For one thing it can be made ahead and transports well, secondly no one suspects it is gluten-free and everyone loves it, even those who sneer at following a gluten-free lifestyle. But most important it is just so fabulous.

CRUST

1¼ cups salted dry roasted peanuts

½ cup granulated sugar

4 tablespoons (½ stick) unsalted butter, melted

6 ounces semisweet chocolate chips

¼ cup heavy whipping cream

2 tablespoons cornstarch

Pinch of kosher or fine sea salt

4 ounces cream cheese, cut in pieces

¾ cup creamy peanut butter

1 teaspoon pure vanilla extract

FILLING

¾ cup whole milk

¾ cup half-and-half

2 large eggs

1 cup confectioners' sugar

TOPPING

1¼ cups heavy whipping cream

2 teaspoons confectioners' sugar

1 ounce semisweet or bittersweet bar chocolate for grating on top, optional

Preheat the oven to 350 degrees.

Put the peanuts and sugar in the food processor and pulse until ground.

Serves 8

Pulse in the melted butter. Press the mixture evenly into the bottom of a 9-inch springform pan, making sure to even it out.

Bake the crust 15 minutes. It will start to brown and be fairly set, but it will still be a little soft when it comes out of the oven; don't worry, it will firm up. Set aside to cool slightly.

While the crust cools, in a microwave-safe bowl, melt the chocolate and cream together in microwave, stirring every 30 seconds until smooth and glossy, 1 to 2 minutes. Or melt the chocolate in a heatproof bowl over a saucepan of barely simmering water, stirring often until melted and glossy. Spread the chocolate mixture over the crust and put the crust in the freezer for about 30 minutes while making the filling.

Whisk the milk, half-and-half, eggs, confectioners' sugar, cornstarch, and salt in a medium saucepan. Cook over medium heat, whisking constantly, until it becomes the consistency of pudding, 5 or 6 minutes. Take the pan off the heat and whisk in the cream cheese, peanut butter, and the vanilla. Let cool slightly. Spread the filling evenly over the chocolate-covered crust and refrigerate for 4 hours, or until cold. The filling can be made a day ahead.

When the pie is cold, remove from the refrigerator, and run a knife around the edges of the springform pan but do not loosen the outer ring.

Prepare the topping. Whip the cream with the confectioners' sugar and spread over the cold pie. After spreading with the cream, it is best to chill the pie for about 30 minutes but not necessary.

Remove the outer ring of the springform pan and place the pie on a serving platter. Grate some chocolate over the top for a pretty presentation, if desired.

Key Lime Pie

Key limes are small, yellowish limes that are tarter than regular limes. Since living in Florida I have discovered that almost every local restaurant, diner, or dive has its own version of key lime pie. There is something about eating this pie that still makes me feel like I am on vacation.

The macadamia nuts in the crust emphasize the tropical flair of this dessert, but it is equally good using all peanuts instead of a combination.

If you can't find fresh key limes, use bottled key lime juice or, in a pinch, freshly squeezed regular lime juice.

CRUST
¾ cup salted, dry-roasted
  peanuts
½ cup salted, dry-roasted
  macadamia nuts
½ cup granulated sugar
4 tablespoons (½ stick) unsalted
  butter, melted

FILLING
4 large egg yolks
Zest of 1 regular lime, finely
  grated

One 14-ounce can sweetened
  condensed milk
⅔ cup freshly squeezed key lime
  juice

TOPPING
1¼ cups heavy cream
2 teaspoons confectioners'
  sugar
½ teaspoon pure vanilla extract
1 regular lime or 2 to 3 key limes
  thinly sliced for garnish

Preheat the oven to 325 degrees.

Put the peanuts, macadamia nuts, and sugar in food processor and pulse until ground. Pulse in the melted butter. Press the mixture evenly into the bottom of a 9-inch springform pan, making sure you even it out.

Bake the crust for 15 minutes. It will start to brown and be fairly set, but

will still be a little soft when it comes out of the oven; don't worry, it will firm up. Set aside to cool slightly. Leave the oven on.

While the crust cools make the filling. In an electric mixer fitted with the wire whisk attachment, whip the egg yolks and lime zest at high speed until fluffy, 5 to 6 minutes. Gradually add the condensed milk and continue to whip until thick, 3 to 4 minutes more. Lower the mixer speed, slowly add the lime juice, and mix until incorporated. Pour the mixture into the cooled crust.

Bake the pie for 15 minutes, or until the filling has just set. Cool on a wire rack for 10 minutes, then refrigerate for at least 30 minutes.

When the pie has cooled, remove it from the refrigerator, and run a knife around the edges of the springform pan but do not loosen the outer ring.

Prepare the topping. Whip the cream with the confectioners' sugar and vanilla and spread over the cold pie; it is best to place the pie in the freezer for 20 minutes just prior to serving but is not necessary.

Remove the outer ring of the springform pan and place the pie on a serving platter. Garnish with the lime slices.

Caramel Apple Tart

My new daughter-in-law Sarah has often expressed an interest in expanding her repertoire of recipes. When she told me she loved apple tarts I wanted to come up with an easy recipe for her that was also a showstopper. This is a sophisticated tart version of caramel apples.

Preparing the recipe in a tart pan makes for an elegant presentation but it can also be made in a 9-inch pie pan (not deep dish), which is even easier; just be sure to layer (not dump) the apples into the pie pan.

CRUST
1 recipe Perfect Pie Crust
   (page 137)

FILLING
8 medium apples (about 2³/₄
   pounds) peeled, cored, and
   sliced into ¹/₂- to ³/₄-inch
   slices
Juice of 1 lemon
1 cup firmly packed light brown
   sugar

¹/₂ teaspoon kosher or fine sea
   salt
1 tablespoon unsalted butter,
   melted

CARAMEL SAUCE
¹/₄ cup firmly packed light brown
   sugar
¹/₄ cup heavy whipping cream
Tiny pinch kosher or fine sea salt
1 tablespoon unsalted butter

Preheat the oven to 375 degrees. Lightly spray an 11-inch tart pan with a removable bottom with gluten-free, nonstick cooking spray. Line a baking sheet with aluminum foil.

Prepare the pie crust according to the recipe directions. Following the rolling method in the recipe, roll out the dough into a circle about 13 inches in diameter. Gently transfer the dough to the prepared tart pan. If the dough cracks just pinch it together. Wrap two sheets of aluminum foil around the

outside of the tart pan. This will keep your oven clean as the caramel tends to seep out while the tart is baking.

Put the sliced apples in a large mixing bowl and squeeze in the lemon juice. Toss to coat. Add the brown sugar and salt. Mix until the apples are completely coated with the brown sugar. Arrange the apples in a circle around the outer edge of the pan, overlapping each other slightly. Continue to arrange the apples in concentric circles, working toward the center of the pan. Make sure the apples fit snugly. Pour the juices accumulated in the bowl over the apples and drizzle on the melted butter.

Bake the tart for 55 to 65 minutes, or until the apples are tender when pierced with a knife. Check the tart after 35 minutes, once the crust and the tips of the apple slices have browned, lay a sheet of foil over the top of the tart, and continue baking. Let the tart cool in the pan for 10 minutes, then remove the foil and outer ring of the tart pan and continue cooling on a wire rack. If the tart cools too much before removing the outer ring of the pan, the caramel will harden making it difficult to get the tart out of the pan. If this happens, simply put the tart in a warm oven (300 degrees) for 5 minutes and it should release. While the tart cools, make the caramel sauce.

In a small saucepan over medium heat, bring all the caramel sauce ingredients to a boil. Stir to dissolve the brown sugar. Continue cooking until the sauce is thick enough to coat the back of a spoon, about 5 minutes. Let the sauce cool slightly then drizzle on top of the tart.

Serve the tart warm or at room temperature.

Easy French Pear Tart

Classic French pear tarts combine poached pears over an almond cream in a pastry shell. This is a simpler version, which eliminates the pastry shell. The batter for this tart forms both the crust and the almond cream. To make it even simpler, use canned pear halves.

If you do decide to poach your own pears, use ripe but firm pears and don't throw out the poaching liquid. You can add a tablespoon or two of the cooled liquid to champagne or sparkling water for a wonderful drink or use it to sweeten iced tea.

PEARS
4 cups water

1¼ cups granulated sugar

Juice of 1 lemon

4 medium Bosc pears, or 8 canned pear halves, drained

ALMOND CREAM
12 tablespoons (1½ sticks) unsalted butter, at room temperature

¾ cup confectioners' sugar

3 large eggs, at room temperature

¾ teaspoon pure vanilla extract

¾ teaspoon pure almond extract

1½ cups blanched almond flour

1 tablespoon plus ½ teaspoon cornstarch

½ teaspoon kosher or fine sea salt

Put the water, sugar, and lemon juice in a large saucepan and stir to combine. Peel the pears with a vegetable peeler, leaving them whole. Place the pears in the liquid and bring to a boil over medium-high heat. Once the water starts to boil, lower the heat and simmer for 15 to 20 minutes, or until the pears can be pierced with the tip of a paring knife. Take the pears off the heat and let them cool in the liquid for 1 to 2 hours.

Preheat the oven to 350 degrees. Lightly spray an 11-inch tart pan, with a removable bottom, with gluten-free, nonstick cooking spray.

In the bowl of an electric mixer fitted with the paddle attachment, cream the butter and sugar on medium speed until light and fluffy, about 3 minutes. Turn the speed to low, and add the eggs, one at a time, mixing until each egg is fully incorporated, scraping down the sides of the bowl with a spatula after each addition. Add the vanilla and almond extracts and mix well.

In a separate large mixing bowl, whisk together the almond flour, cornstarch, and salt. Add the flour mixture to the butter mixture and mix well. With a large spatula scrape down the sides and bottom of the bowl well to make sure all the ingredients are combined. Pour the batter into the prepared pan and smooth the top with an offset spatula.

If using poached pears, cut the pears in half lengthwise and remove the stems, and using a small melon baller, remove the cores. Regardless of whether you use poached or canned pears make sure you dry the pear halves very well. Lay the pears cut side down on a cutting board and, using a paring knife, slice them lengthwise in about ¼-inch slices almost to the top, but leaving them attached at the very top. Gently push down on the pears to fan them out slightly. Using a spatula, gently lift the pears and place on the almond cream with the widest part of the pear toward the edge of the pan.

Place the tart pan on a baking sheet and bake for 35 to 45 minutes, or until the crust is golden brown and the almond cream is set. Let cool in pan for 15 minutes, then remove the outer ring of the tart pan, place the tart on a wire rack, and let cool completely.

Serves 8 to 10

Fig and Goat Cheese Tarts

**Makes eight
4-inch tarts**

This is a gorgeous dessert when fresh figs are in season. Topped with a drizzle of honey, these tarts will wow guests. Use Black Mission or Brown Turkey figs for the best result. Use tart pans with removable bottoms for a pretty presentation.

CRUST
1 recipe Tart Shell (page 140)

FILLING
16 ounces goat cheese
2 large eggs
½ cup plus 2 tablespoons sugar

2 teaspoons freshly squeezed lemon juice
1 teaspoon pure vanilla extract
2 pounds fresh figs
2 to 3 tablespoons honey

Preheat the oven to 350 degrees.

Prepare the tart shell dough according to the recipe directions. Roll out the dough between two sheets of parchment paper, until large enough to cut into eight 6-inch circles. Cut into circles and transfer to the tart pans. If the dough tears while cutting or transferring just pinch it back together. Line the dough with pieces of parchment paper and fill with dried beans, rice, or pie weights. Prebake the tart shells for 15 minutes, or until they are lightly browned. Remove the shells from the oven and let cool. Leave the oven on.

While the crusts are baking and cooling, prepare the filling. In an electric mixer fitted with the paddle attachment, beat the goat cheese on medium speed until smooth. Add the eggs, sugar, lemon juice, and vanilla and beat until smooth and well combined. Divide the mixture evenly among the prebaked tart shells. Bake for 15 minutes, or until the filling is set but not dry. Let the tarts cool in the pans for 10 to 15 minutes, then refrigerate until cold, about 1 hour.

Prior to serving, remove the tarts from the pans, slice the figs in quarters lengthwise, and place them on top of the filling in concentric circles. Drizzle with a little honey and serve.

Lemon Tart

A buttery shortbread crust filled with tart lemon curd is such a classic dessert to end a meal.

The lemon curd in this recipe is also fabulous spread on gluten-free English muffins for breakfast, poured into a meringue pie crust, or spooned over fresh fruit. It can be made two to three weeks ahead and stored in a covered container in the refrigerator.

To vary the recipe, substitute equal amounts of lime or orange for the lemon in this recipe.

CRUST
One 11-inch or six 4-inch Shortbread Tart Crust(s), baked and
cooled (page 141)

LEMON CURD
8 tablespoons (1 stick)
unsalted butter, at room
temperature
1¹/₂ cups granulated sugar

4 tablespoons lemon zest (about
4 lemons), finely grated
4 large eggs, at room temperature
¹/₂ cup freshly squeezed lemon
juice
Pinch of kosher or fine sea salt
Candied Citrus Peels (page 126)
for garnish, optional

Prepare the shortbread tart crust(s) according to the recipe directions. Bake and cool.

In the bowl of an electric mixer fitted with the paddle attachment, cream the butter with the sugar and lemon zest on medium-high speed until smooth, about 1 minute. Turn mixer to low speed and add the eggs, one at a time, mixing well and scraping down the sides of the bowl after each addition. Add the lemon juice and salt and mix until combined.

Pour the mixture into a large saucepan and cook over low heat, stirring constantly, until thickened, 8 to 10 minutes; the mixture needs to come just to

a simmer before it will thicken up. Remove from heat and let cool slightly. Pour the lemon curd into the baked and cooled tart shell(s). Let sit at room temperature until the curd has cooled and set.

Garnish with candied citrus peels, if using.

Both the tart shell and lemon curd can be made in advance. If you do this, refrigerate the curd until ready to use. The tart shell(s) can be made a day ahead and stored, wrapped in plastic wrap, at room temperature. Fill the tart shell with the curd just before serving.

Raspberry Tart

This is an easy, elegant dessert and I just love these tarts with the raspberries all lined up like little soldiers. For an even more intense berry flavor, prepare the berry pastry cream variation using frozen raspberries.

Serve the tart as is or sprinkle a light dusting of confectioners' sugar over the berries just before serving.

Serves 6 to 8

CRUST
One 11-inch or six 4-inch Shortbread Tart Crust(s), baked and
cooled (page 141)

FILLING
1 recipe Pastry Cream
(page 188) or Berry Pastry
Cream (page 189)

½ cup good-quality raspberry
preserves

TOPPING
2 pints fresh raspberries
Confectioners' sugar for dusting,
optional

Prepare the shortbread Tart Crust(s) according to the recipe directions. Bake and cool.

Prepare the pastry cream and refrigerate until cold. Whisk well.

Spread the raspberry preserves over the bottom of the baked and cooled tart shell(s) and fill with the pastry cream.

Just prior to serving, place the raspberries on the tart, stem side down, starting in the center and working out to the edge in concentric circles. Dust with confectioners' sugar, if desired.

The pastry cream and tart shell(s) can be prepared ahead of time. Keep the pastry cream refrigerated until ready to fill the tart. The tart shell(s) can be made a day ahead and stored, wrapped in plastic wrap, at room temperature.

Mocha Cream Tart

Serves 6 to 8

A buttery, chocolate shortbread crust filled with mocha pastry cream, topped with a cloud of lightly whipped cream—what more can I say? I can happily skip dinner and get straight to the dessert.

CRUST

One 11-inch or six 4-inch Chocolate Shortbread Tart Crust(s), baked and cooled (page 142)

FILLING

1 recipe Mocha Pastry Cream (page 189)

1½ cups heavy whipping cream

Grated chocolate, chocolate shards (page 241), or cocoa powder for garnish, optional

Prepare mocha pastry cream and refrigerate until cold. Whisk well. Whip the heavy cream until stiff peaks form. Whisk one-third of the whipped cream gently into the mocha pastry cream.

Fill the baked and cooled tart shell(s) with the pastry cream and top with the remaining whipped cream.

Garnish with grated chocolate, chocolate shards, or a dusting of cocoa powder, if desired.

The pastry cream and tart shell(s) can be prepared ahead of time. Keep the pastry cream refrigerated until just before serving then add the whipped cream and fill the tart shell(s). The tart shell(s) can be made a day ahead and stored, wrapped in plastic wrap, at room temperature.

Chocolate Orange Tarts

These tarts are a perfect example of how mastering a few basic recipes opens the door to all sorts of possibilities. When testing my recipe for chocolate short-bread tart crusts, I had an extra batch sitting there begging to be filled and eaten. I stirred a bit of orange zest and Grand Marnier into some pastry cream, topped them with candied orange slices and voilà, elegant, dinner party-appropriate tarts with a classic flavor combination of orange and chocolate.

Serves 6

CRUST
Six 4-inch Chocolate Shortbread
　　Tart Crusts (1 recipe), baked
　　and cooled (page 142)

FILLING
1 recipe Orange Pastry Cream
　　(page 189)

½ cup heavy whipping
　　cream
Candied orange slices (page 126),
　　grated chocolate, chocolate
　　shards (page 241), or cocoa
　　powder for garnish, optional

Prepare the orange pastry cream and refrigerate until cold. Whisk well. Whip the heavy cream until stiff peaks form and whisk gently into the orange pastry cream.

Fill the baked and cooled tart crusts with the pastry cream.

Garnish each tart with a candied orange slice or grated chocolate, chocolate shards, or a dusting of cocoa powder.

The pastry cream and tart crusts can be prepared ahead of time. Keep the pastry cream refrigerated until just before serving then add the whipped cream and fill the tart crusts. The tart crusts can be made a day ahead and stored, wrapped in plastic wrap, at room temperature.

Chocolate Galette

A galette is a rustic, free-form pastry typically filled with fruit. For a change of pace try this delicious chocolate version. It could almost be called a chocolate pizza and like pizza, the toppings can be changed to suit your tastes—chopped dried cherries or apricots would be fabulous.

CRUST

1 recipe Perfect Pie Crust (chocolate variation) (page 139)

FILLING

1 cup bittersweet chocolate chips

1 teaspoon instant espresso powder

2 large egg whites

$\frac{1}{8}$ teaspoon kosher or fine sea salt

$\frac{1}{4}$ cup sugar

1 teaspoon pure vanilla extract

$\frac{3}{4}$ cup shelled, salted pistachios, roughly chopped

One 1-ounce square white chocolate, at room temperature

Preheat the oven to 350 degrees. Line a baking sheet with parchment paper.

Prepare the chocolate variation of the Perfect Pie Crust according to the recipe directions. Following the rolling method in the recipe, roll out the dough into an oval about 13 inches by 9 inches and about ¼ inch thick. Transfer the rolled dough to the prepared baking sheet. Brush off any excess flour. Roll and fold the edge of the dough over to form a rimmed crust. Bake for 15 minutes, or until the dough is fairly firm. Leave the oven on.

In a microwave-safe bowl, melt the chocolate in the microwave for about 2 minutes, or until most of the chocolate is melted, stirring every 20 seconds. Or place the chocolate chips in a heatproof bowl over a saucepan with an inch or two of barely simmering water, stirring occasionally until melted; the bottom of the bowl should not touch the water. Stir in the espresso powder and continue stirring until all the chocolate is melted. Let cool slightly.

Beat the egg whites and salt in the bowl of an electric mixer fitted with the whisk attachment until foamy, starting on low speed and increasing to high. Gradually add the sugar and beat until stiff peaks form. Add the vanilla and mix well. Fold the chocolate into the egg whites until the mixture is no longer streaky. Spread the filling evenly over the baked crust, it should be about ½ inch thick. Sprinkle the chopped pistachios over the top.

Return the galette to the oven and bake for another 10 minutes, or until the filling looks a bit dry and has cracked slightly. Let cool on the pan for 5 minutes, then transfer to a wire rack to finish cooling.

Once the galette has cooled, drag a vegetable peeler across the side of the white chocolate square and let the curls of chocolate fall over the top of the galette. Serve slightly warm or cool. Can be made a day ahead, covered with plastic wrap, and stored in the refrigerator.

Apricot Almond Tart

Serves 8 to 10

The base of this tart is an almond mixture that is not too sweet and really lets the apricots shine. Best of all, it is easy to prepare, and the oven does most of the work. For a variation try peaches or sweet plums.

6 tablespoons (³/₄ stick) melted, unsalted butter or nondairy butter substitute, cooled slightly plus more for preparing the pan

3 tablespoons confectioners' sugar plus more for preparing the pan and dusting the top

1³/₄ cups ground almond meal

3 large eggs, slightly beaten

Pinch of kosher or fine sea salt

¹/₄ cup honey

1 teaspoon pure vanilla extract

1 teaspoon pure almond extract

8 large fresh apricots, halved, pitted, and then halved again (if not in season canned apricots will work fine, cut each half in half again)

Preheat the oven to 350 degrees. Grease a 9-inch springform pan with butter or nondairy butter substitute and then dust with confectioners' sugar, tapping out the excess.

In a large mixing bowl combine the melted butter, confectioners' sugar, ground almonds, eggs, salt, honey, and the extracts. Mix very well with a whisk until there are no lumps. Pour the mixture into the prepared pan.

Arrange the apricots in concentric circles on top of the batter, being careful not to overcrowd the center for even baking. You want the edges of the apricots to stick out of the batter a bit.

Bake the tart for 40 to 50 minutes, or until browned and set. Rotate the pan a quarter-turn twice during baking to ensure even browning.

Let the tart cool, then remove from the springform pan. Dust with additional confectioners' sugar. Serve warm or at room temperature.

S'Mores

• Grain-free

When I was a kid I wanted to be a Girl Scout for one reason and one reason only—I heard they went camping and made s'mores.

No need to brave the elements to enjoy these classic campfire treats. If you bake these little tarts in silicone muffin cups they can be unmolded, making for an elegant presentation.

CRUST

1½ cups blanched almond flour

2 tablespoons sugar

¼ cup honey

3 tablespoons unsalted butter, melted

¼ teaspoon kosher or fine sea salt

9 tablespoons (1 stick plus 1 table-spoon) unsalted butter

3 tablespoons sugar

3 tablespoons heavy whipping cream

3 large eggs

FILLING

6 ounces semisweet chocolate chips

1 recipe Marshmallow Frosting (page 86)

Preheat the oven to 350 degrees. Insert muffin papers or silicone baking cups in 12 standard-size muffin cups.

Combine all the ingredients for the crust in a mixing bowl. Divide the mixture evenly among the prepared muffin cups. Bake the crusts for 13 to 15 minutes, or until they are lightly browned. Set aside while preparing the filling. Leave the oven on.

Place the chocolate chips in a medium heatproof bowl and set aside.

Put the butter, sugar, and cream in a small saucepan and bring just to a boil over medium heat. Pour the mixture over the chocolate and set aside, undisturbed, for 2 to 3 minutes. Gently whisk until smooth. Add the eggs, one at a

**Makes 12
S'mores**

time, whisking quickly until the mixture is smooth. Divide the filling evenly among the baked crusts and bake for 15 minutes, or until set. Let cool completely in the pan.

Preheat the broiler to its highest setting. Spoon or pipe marshmallow frosting onto the cooled filling in big swirls. Place the muffin pan under the broiler and broil the s'mores just until the frosting is nicely browned, about a minute or two. Watch carefully, as it goes from not browned to burnt in seconds.

Apricot Dacquoise

A dacquoise is a French dessert made with meringue to which ground nuts have been added and layered with buttercream frosting.

I recall seeing Julia Child make a rectangular dacquoise on a cooking show where she mentioned that the great thing about the shape was that you could always slice off the end and eat it, then re-ice the cake with extra buttercream, and your guests would be none the wiser—yet another reason why I love Julia Child.

Julia's version was a complicated affair with piped meringues, steeped dried apricots run through a food mill, and boozy buttercream beat over an ice bath. My version is simplified; I bake the meringues in cake pans to avoid the piping and add apricot preserves to a quick buttercream. For a taste closer to what I imagine Julia's to be like, use orange liqueur in the buttercream instead of the cream.

MERINGUES

3 egg whites

1/8 teaspoon cream of tartar

1/8 teaspoon kosher or fine sea salt

3/4 cup granulated sugar

1/2 teaspoon pure vanilla extract

1/4 teaspoon pure almond extract

1 1/2 cups blanched almonds, ground or very finely chopped

BUTTERCREAM

1 1/2 cups confectioners' sugar

8 tablespoons (1 stick) unsalted butter, at room temperature

Pinch of kosher or fine sea salt

1/2 teaspoon pure vanilla extract

2 teaspoons freshly squeezed lemon juice

2 to 4 teaspoons heavy whipping cream or orange liqueur

1/2 cup apricot preserves

1/2 to 3/4 cup sliced almonds for decoration

Preheat the oven to 300 degrees. Lightly spray three 9-inch cake pans with gluten-free, nonstick cooking spray.

Serves 8

In an electric mixer fitted with the whisk attachment, beat the egg whites at medium speed until they start to foam. With the mixer still running, add the cream of tartar and salt. Turn the speed to high and gradually add the sugar. Continue beating until stiff peaks form and the sugar is completely dissolved. Test this by rubbing some of the egg white mixture between your thumb and forefinger. If it is smooth and no longer feels gritty, the sugar is dissolved. Turn off mixer, add the vanilla and almond extracts, turn the mixer back on to high, and mix until the extracts are fully incorporated. Fold in the 1½ cups ground almonds.

Divide the meringue batter evenly among the three prepared pans, smoothing the top with a spatula. Bake for 40 to 45 minutes, or until the meringues are firm and lightly browned. Let cool in the pans for 1 hour. While the meringues are cooling make the buttercream.

In an electric mixer fitted with the wire whisk attachment, whisk together the confectioners' sugar, butter, and salt starting on low speed and gradually increasing to medium. Continue beating for 3 minutes. Add the vanilla, lemon juice, and 2 teaspoons of cream or orange liqueur and whisk for 1 more minute, adding more cream or liqueur, if necessary, until a creamy, spreadable consistency is achieved. With a spatula, fold in the apricot preserves. Refrigerate the buttercream until ready to use.

Remove the meringues from the pans by flipping them over onto a countertop and gently rapping the pan until they fall out.

To assemble, place one meringue on a serving platter. Spread a little less than one-third of the buttercream over the meringue, top with another meringue, more buttercream, and finally the last meringue. Frost the top and sides with the remaining buttercream.

Decorate the *dacquoise* by patting the sliced almonds around the sides, sticking them to the buttercream. Refrigerate the *dacquoise* until serving time.

Red, White, and Blue Pavlova

ᘓᘐᘓᘐᘓᘐᘓᘐᘓᘐᘓᘐᘓᘐᘓᘐᘓᘐᘓᘐᘓᘐᘓᘐ

There are a lot of things to love about Australia; the spectacular Sydney Harbor, the Great Barrier Reef, my fabulous friend Jude, and pavlova!

Pavlova is a dessert every gluten-free cook should have in their dessert repertoire. It is naturally gluten-free, easy to make, and utterly delicious.

I decided to make an all-American pavlova for the Fourth of July. Decked out in red, white, and blue this native Australian can become a new American classic.

• Grain-free

4 large egg whites, at room temperature

Pinch of kosher or fine sea salt

1 cup granulated sugar

2 teaspoons cornstarch

1 teaspoon white vinegar

1 teaspoon pure vanilla extract

1 cup cold, heavy whipping cream

1 tablespoon confectioners' sugar

½ pint fresh raspberries

1 pint fresh blueberries

Preheat the oven to 180 degrees.

Draw a 9-inch circle on one side of a piece of parchment paper, using a cake or pie pan as a guide. Flip the parchment over so the circle is on the reverse side and place on a sheet pan.

Beat the egg whites with the salt in a large mixing bowl until they start to firm up, about 1 minute. With the mixer going slowly add the sugar and continue to beat until it forms firm, shiny peaks, about 2 minutes. Remove the bowl from the mixer.

Sift the cornstarch onto the egg whites and add the vinegar and vanilla, folding lightly with a spatula. Pile the egg white mixture onto the parchment paper in the center of the traced circle. Gently spread the mixture to fill the circle, starting from the middle and working out in all directions. Just even it out slightly; you do not want it to be perfectly smooth or to overwork it.

Bake the pavlova for 1½ hours and then turn off the oven and let cool completely in the oven, about 2 hours.

Serves 6 to 8

Beat the heavy whipping cream with the confectioners' sugar until it forms soft peaks. Do not overbeat.

When the pavlova is completely cool, peel off the parchment paper and place the pavlova on a plate or serving platter. Spread the whipped cream evenly over the pavlova leaving about a ½-inch border of meringue, then ring the whipped cream with the raspberries, and fill the center with the blueberries.

Chocolate Pavlova with Raspberry Cream

෬෬෬෬෬෬෬෬෬෬෬෬෬෬෬෬෬෬෬෬෬෬෬෬෬෬෬෬෬෬

Crisp on the outside and chocolatly-marshmallowy on the inside, this chocolate pavlova is piled with raspberry cream and topped with fresh berries. It is an impressive dessert that requires a little time but very little effort.

• Grain-free

4 large egg whites, at room temperature

1/8 teaspoon cream of tartar

Pinch of kosher or fine sea salt

1 cup plus 2 teaspoons granulated sugar

1 1/2 teaspoons cornstarch

1 teaspoon pure vanilla extract

1 tablespoon white vinegar

1/2 cup dark, unsweetened Dutch-processed cocoa powder

1 cup frozen raspberries, thawed

1 cup heavy whipping cream

1 pint fresh berries such as raspberries, blackberries, or strawberries or a combination

Cocoa powder for dusting, optional

Preheat the oven to 300 degrees.

Draw a 9-inch circle on one side of a piece of parchment paper, using a cake or pie pan as a guide. Flip the parchment paper over so the circle is on the reverse side and place on a baking sheet.

In the bowl of an electric mixer fitted with the whisk attachment, beat the egg whites with the cream of tartar and salt on medium speed until foamy and the cream of tartar is fully incorporated, about 30 seconds. With the mixer running, gradually add 1 cup of the sugar. Turn the mixer off; add the cornstarch, vanilla, and vinegar. Turn the mixer back on, increasing the speed to high and beat until the mixture is glossy and stiff peaks form, 3 to 5 minutes. Remove the bowl from the mixer.

Sift the cocoa powder into the egg white mixture and fold it in with a large spatula until the mixture is well combined and no longer streaky. Pile the mixture on to the parchment paper in the center of the traced circle. Gently spread

Serves 6 to 8

the mixture with the spatula to fill the circle, starting in the middle and working out in all directions. Just even it out slightly; you do not want it perfectly smooth or to overwork it. Bake the pavlova for 10 minutes, reduce the oven temperature to 300 degrees and continue to bake for 40 to 45 minutes, or until it is dry and firm. Turn off the oven but leave the pavlova in the oven to dry for at least 30 minutes or up to 2 hours.

Put the thawed raspberries in a blender with 2 teaspoons of granulated sugar and blend until smooth, about 30 seconds. Push the mixture through a fine strainer to remove the seeds.

Whip the cream until soft peaks form. Fold in the strained raspberry sauce.

To serve, place the pavlova on a serving dish, pile on the whipped cream, and spread to about 1 inch from the edge. Top with fresh berries, dust with additional cocoa powder, if desired, and serve.

Peach Cobbler

When peaches are ripe and juicy it is definitely time to make this Southern classic. I think this is my family's all-time favorite comfort dessert. Of course fresh peaches, perfectly ripe are the best, but if it's the dead of winter, or you just don't feel like peeling and slicing you can substitute canned peaches. If using peaches canned in syrup, cut the sugar in half (in the peach liquid) and use the can's liquid instead of water.

The best way to eat this dessert is warm from the oven with a bit of cream poured on top.

PEACHES

8 medium peaches, peeled, pitted, and sliced (about 8 cups)

Juice of 1 lemon

2 tablespoons packed light brown sugar

2 tablespoons granulated sugar

¼ cup water

1 teaspoon pure vanilla extract

2 teaspoons cornstarch

2 tablespoons unsalted butter

COBBLER CRUST

1½ cups sweet rice flour blend

½ cup plus 2 teaspoons granulated sugar

2 teaspoons baking powder

½ teaspoon baking soda

½ teaspoon kosher or fine sea salt

8 tablespoons (1 stick) cold, unsalted butter, cut into small pieces

¾ cup buttermilk

Preheat the oven to 375 degrees.

Toss the peaches with the lemon juice, brown and granulated sugars, water, vanilla, and cornstarch until the peaches are well coated. Set aside while you make the cobbler crust.

In a large mixing bowl, whisk together the sweet rice flour blend, ½ cup granulated sugar, baking powder, baking soda, and salt. Cut in the butter using a pastry cutter or your fingertips, until the mixture resembles coarse crumbs.

Serves 8 to 10

Add the buttermilk and stir until just combined; the batter will be a soft, wet dough.

In a 10-inch, cast-iron skillet, melt the remaining 2 tablespoons of butter over medium heat. Add the peaches along with any juices that have accumulated in the bowl to the skillet and cook until the peaches are warm and the sauce is bubbly, about 5 minutes, stirring occasionally. Drop the cobbler crust dough by tablespoonfuls onto the warm peaches, leaving small gaps between. Sprinkle the remaining 2 teaspoons of granulated sugar over the dough.

Bake the cobbler for 35 to 45 minutes, or until the cobbler crust is browned and the peaches are bubbly. Let cool slightly and serve.

Strawberry Rhubarb Crumble

Makes eight
8-ounce
servings

This is an everyday dessert that can be thrown together in a hurry using frozen fruit, the ideal treat for hectic days. For extra indulgence top with a scoop of vanilla ice cream or some lightly whipped cream.

The addition of the liqueur is optional but, in my opinion, elevates this humble dessert from everyday to special. And honestly, don't we deserve to feel special every day?

STRAWBERRY RHUBARB MIXTURE

One 16-ounce bag frozen strawberries

One 16-ounce bag frozen cut rhubarb

4 teaspoons cornstarch

3 tablespoons sugar

2 tablespoons crème de cassis, Chambord, or any other fruit flavored liqueur (optional)

CRUMBLE TOPPING

³/₄ cup sweet rice flour blend

¹/₂ cup gluten-free oats

¹/₂ cup sugar

¹/₂ teaspoon kosher or fine sea salt

8 tablespoons (1 stick) unsalted butter, melted

Place frozen fruit in a mixing bowl, sprinkle on the cornstarch, 3 tablespoons of sugar, and the liqueur and give it all a toss. Spoon mixture into eight 8-ounce ramekins or one 10-inch round baking dish.

Make the topping by whisking together the sweet rice flour blend, oats, ¹/₂ cup sugar, and salt. Add the melted butter and stir with a spatula or spoon until all the dry ingredients have been moistened with the butter. Crumble the topping over the strawberry rhubarb mixture. Bake for 35 to 45 minutes or until the fruit is bubbly and the toppings have browned. Serve warm.

Pâte à Choux (Cream Puff Dough)

• Sugar-free

Baked and filled, this versatile dough can become cream puffs or éclairs. Filled with ice cream and topped with chocolate sauce cream puffs become profiteroles. Fry it, and you get beignets, or doughnuts.

An old recipe book I own describes a labor-intensive method which involves seemingly endless stirring with a wooden spoon and piping with a pastry bag (something I have never seemed to master). It was enough to keep me from trying my hand at pâte à choux, cream puff dough, for years. Modern kitchen equipment eliminates most of the work and this dough is actually very simple to make.

The hallmark of a good cream puff or éclair is that it is crispy and browned on the outside and light and airy inside. If, despite all your best efforts, you find some doughy bits inside of your pastry just pull it out with your fingers and toss it. No one will be the wiser and it just leaves more room for filling, which can't be a bad thing!

Be sure to gather all your ingredients before you start, and have your mixer or food processor ready to go.

4 large eggs
8 tablespoons (1 stick) unsalted
   butter
1 cup water

Pinch of kosher or fine sea
   salt
1 cup sweet rice flour blend

Crack the eggs into a liquid measuring cup or pitcher.

In a medium saucepan, combine the butter, water, and salt and bring just to a boil over medium heat, giving the pan a swirl, or stir occasionally to help the butter along with melting. As soon as the water comes to a boil, turn the heat down to low and dump in the sweet rice flour blend all at once. Stir quickly and in one direction with a wooden spoon. The liquid will start absorbing the flour and will form into a ball. Continue cooking and stirring for 1 or 2 minutes to cook off some of the liquid. The pan will start to coat with a film of butter.

Makes 12 to 18
cream puffs or
éclairs depend-
ing on size

Dump the dough into the bowl of a standing mixer fitted with the paddle attachment, or use a food processor (see below) and beat the dough for about 1 minute on medium speed to cool it off slightly. Add the eggs, one at a time, mixing until each egg is fully incorporated before adding the next. Continue mixing until the dough is thick and shiny, about 3 minutes.

If you are using a food processor, dump the dough into the machine, process for 30 seconds, and then start adding the eggs, one at a time, through the feed tube. Let the machine whirl for a few seconds to fully incorporate each egg before adding the next. Once all the eggs have been incorporated let the machine go for about 30 seconds more.

Preheat the oven to 425 degrees while preparing the dough. Line baking sheets with parchment paper or silicone baking mats.

To make cream puffs (*choux*), using a small ice cream scoop, scoop mounds of the dough onto the prepared pans, spacing them about 1 inch apart. If the dough spreads out more than you would like, just moisten your fingers with water and shape them up.

If you are proficient with a pastry bag, the dough can be piped into little puffs for cream puffs or into strips for éclairs. For cream puffs, pipe the dough onto the prepared sheets in mounds about 1½ inches in diameter by about 1 inch high. Wet your finger and press down the little peaks on the top as they will burn. For éclairs, pipe into strips 3 to 4 inches long.

Bake the pastries for 20 minutes, or until lightly browned; the baking time may be shorter or longer depending on the size. Turn off the oven but leave the pastries in the oven for another 20 minutes to dry out. The puffs or éclairs should be golden brown and sound hollow when tapped on the bottom. Remove from oven and pierce the side of each cream puff or éclair with a small, sharp knife to let the steam escape. Let cool completely.

Cut the pastries in half horizontally and fill with whipped cream, pastry cream, ice cream, jam, or anything else you wish.

Dairy-free Cream Puffs

• Dairy-free

When I started experimenting with making cream puffs I wondered how they would turn out without dairy. After all, the dough is basically water, butter, eggs, and flour. I was not happy with the results when I used dairy-free butter substitute for the butter and found they were flavorless with oil and water. So I tried coconut milk and grapeseed oil and voilà! Perfect. So perfect, in fact, that I actually prefer these babies to the regular ones.

The cream puffs can be frozen after baking, crisped in a 350-degree oven for a few minutes, cooled, and filled before serving. I have even frozen them filled when I had to make dozens for a party. You can let them thaw for about half an hour, or if you forget to thaw them (as I have done) they are terrific frozen as well.

Have all your ingredients ready before starting this recipe.

PASTRY

4 large eggs plus 1 egg yolk
½ cup grapeseed oil
1 cup coconut milk (shake can
  well before measuring)
Pinch of kosher or fine sea salt
1 cup sweet rice flour blend

1 recipe Dairy-Free Pastry Cream
  (page 191)

½ recipe Dairy-Free Chocolate
  Ganache (page 84), or confectioners' sugar for dusting

Preheat the oven to 425 degrees. Line baking sheets with parchment paper or silicone baking mats.

Crack the eggs and egg yolk into a liquid measuring cup or pitcher.

In a medium saucepan, combine the oil, coconut milk, and salt and bring just to a boil over medium heat. Stir to try and incorporate the oil into the coconut milk. It won't completely happen but don't worry. As soon as the mixture comes to a boil, turn the heat down to medium-low and dump in the sweet rice flour blend all at once. Stir quickly and in one direction with a wooden spoon. The liquid will start absorbing the flour and will form into a ball. Continue cooking and stirring for 1 or 2 minutes. You will see that some of the oil is separating out from the dough, but that's fine.

Makes 12 to 18 depending on size

Dump the dough, separated oil and all, into the bowl of a standing mixer fitted with the paddle attachment and beat the dough for about 1 minute on medium speed to cool it off slightly. Add the eggs, one at a time, mixing until each egg is fully incorporated before adding the next. As you are incorporating the eggs, some oil may splatter to the sides of the bowl and it will look like a lumpy, gooey mess. No worries! Continue mixing until the dough is uniformly smooth, thick, and shiny, 3 to 5 minutes.

Using a small ice cream scoop, place mounds of the dough on the prepared pans, spacing them about 1 inch apart. If you are good at piping, then you can pipe little mounds about 1½ inches wide by 1 inch high. Moisten your finger with water and push down the little peaks as they will burn.

Bake the cream puffs for 20 minutes, or until lightly browned; the baking time may be shorter or longer depending on the size. Turn off the oven but leave the pastries in the oven for another 20 minutes to dry out. The puffs should be golden brown and sound hollow when tapped on the bottom. Remove from the oven and pierce the side of each puff with a small, sharp knife to let the steam escape. Let cool completely.

Cut the cream puffs in half horizontally and fill with dairy-free pastry cream.

Top with either dairy-free ganache or dust with some confectioners' sugar.

Pastry Cream

Used to fill tarts, cakes, cream puffs, éclairs, and other pastries, pastry cream is a pastry chef's staple that is well worth learning to make. It is not difficult; the main tricks are to cook the mixture for no more than two minutes after it comes back to a boil or the cornstarch loses its effectiveness, and to strain the mixture through a sieve to remove any lumps for a silken texture. My biggest challenge? Waiting for it to cool; I can't seem to resist eating a spoonful or twelve, warm, straight from the pan.

Pastry cream can be flavored in a variety of ways. I have given a few of my favorite variations below.

2 cups whole milk	3 tablespoons cornstarch
¼ teaspoon kosher or fine sea salt	2 tablespoons cold, unsalted
6 large egg yolks, at room	butter
temperature	1 tablespoon pure vanilla extract
½ cup sugar	

In a large saucepan, bring the milk and salt to a boil, take off the heat, and set aside.

In the bowl of an electric mixer fitted with a paddle attachment, beat the egg yolks and sugar on medium-high speed until the mixture is thick and light yellow, about 3 minutes. Turn the speed to low, and beat in the cornstarch. Then slowly pour the hot milk into the egg mixture and beat until well mixed. Pour the mixture back into the saucepan.

Cook the mixture over medium heat, stirring constantly with a whisk or wooden spoon until the mixture becomes thick and starts to gently boil. Continue to cook for 1 to 2 minutes more. Remove from heat and stir in the cold butter and vanilla. If the mixture appears curdled, just whisk the daylights out of it until it comes together again. Strain the mixture through a fine sieve into a bowl. Cover with a piece of plastic wrap, pressed directly on top of the pastry cream to prevent a skin from forming. Refrigerate until cold, about 2 hours.

The pastry cream can be made 2 to 3 days ahead and stored in the refrigerator. Whisk the pastry cream until smooth before using.

VARIATIONS

Chocolate Pastry Cream: Add 4 ounces melted bittersweet, semisweet, or white chocolate to the hot milk and stir well before adding the hot milk to the egg mixture.

Coffee Pastry Cream: Add 2 tablespoons instant espresso or instant coffee granules to the milk before heating.

If you would like to use Kahlúa for flavoring, reduce the vanilla extract to 1 teaspoon and add 1 tablespoon Kahlúa at the same time.

Mocha Pastry Cream: Add 4 ounces melted bittersweet, semisweet, or white chocolate and 2 tablespoons instant espresso powder or instant coffee granules to the hot milk and stir well before adding to the egg mixture.

Orange Pastry Cream: Add 1 tablespoon orange juice and 1½ teaspoons finely grated orange zest to the basic pastry cream mixture before heating.

Reduce the vanilla extract to 1 teaspoon and stir 1 tablespoon Grand Marnier or other orange-flavored liqueur into the basic pastry cream mixture with the butter and vanilla.

Stir in another 1½ teaspoons finely grated orange zest to the pastry cream after has been strained.

Light Pastry Cream: This my favorite filling for cream puffs. To lighten pastry cream, just before using the cream, whip 1 cup heavy whipping cream until stiff peaks start to form. Whisk the pastry cream until smooth then fold in the whipped cream until fully incorporated.

Berry Pastry Cream: If you would like to flavor pastry cream with Chambord or another berry-flavored liqueur, reduce the vanilla extract to 1 teaspoon and add 1 tablespoon liqueur with the extract.

**Makes about
2½ cups**

Puree ½ cup thawed frozen strawberries or raspberries with 1 tablespoon of sugar in a blender on high speed. Push the puree through a fine strainer to remove seeds. Whisk the cooled pastry cream well, and fold in the berry puree with a spatula until well blended.

Dairy-free Pastry Cream

Coconut milk is the base of this dairy-free pastry cream. The coconut flavor is so subtle that even die-hard coconut haters love pastries filled with this luscious "cream."

Equally as versatile as regular pastry cream this recipe adapts equally well to the variations. Just be sure to use dairy-free chocolate for the chocolate variety.

• Dairy-free

Makes about 2½ cups

2 cups coconut milk (shake the cans well before measuring)

¼ teaspoon kosher or fine sea salt

6 large egg yolks, at room temperature

½ cup sugar

3 tablespoons cornstarch

1½ teaspoons pure vanilla extract

½ teaspoon pure almond extract

In a large saucepan, bring the coconut milk and salt to a boil, take off the heat, and set aside.

In the bowl of an electric mixer fitted with a paddle attachment, beat the egg yolks and sugar on medium-high speed until thick and light yellow, about 3 minutes. Turn the speed to low, and beat in the cornstarch. Then slowly pour the hot coconut milk into the egg mixture and beat until well mixed. Pour the mixture back into the saucepan.

Cook the mixture over medium heat, stirring constantly with a whisk or wooden spoon, until the mixture becomes thick and starts to gently boil. Continue to cook for 1 to 2 minutes more. Remove from heat and stir in the extracts. If the mixture appears curdled, just whisk the daylights out of it until it comes together again. Strain the mixture through a fine sieve into a clean bowl. Cover with a piece of plastic wrap, pressed directly on top of the pastry cream, to prevent a skin from forming. Refrigerate until cold, about 2 hours.

The pastry cream can be made 2 to 3 days ahead and stored in the refrigerator. Whisk the pastry cream until smooth before using.

Puddings and Custards

Cocoa Pudding

Rich, satiny chocolate comfort in a cup, this dessert is like hot cocoa in a cool, pudding form. And what would hot cocoa be without the marshmallows? Making good use of the leftover egg white from the pudding, the marshmallows are really melt in your mouth meringues made by steaming briefly in the microwave and then off for a quick crisp in the oven.

1 large egg, separated

6 tablespoons unsweetened cocoa powder

$^1/_2$ cup granulated sugar

$^1/_4$ cup cornstarch

$^1/_8$ teaspoon kosher or fine sea salt

3 cups whole milk

$^3/_4$ cup semisweet chocolate chips

$1^3/_4$ teaspoons pure vanilla extract

1 teaspoon confectioners' sugar

Place the egg yolk in a large mixing bowl and beat it with a fork. Place the egg white in a medium mixing bowl and set aside.

In a large saucepan, whisk together the cocoa powder, 6 tablespoons of the granulated sugar, cornstarch, and salt. Gradually whisk in the milk. Place over medium heat and bring to a boil. Boil, stirring constantly, for 1 minute.

Gradually pour some of the hot cocoa mixture into the bowl containing the egg yolk and whisk well. Add the rest of the hot cocoa mixture gradually, whisking continuously. Add the chocolate chips and whisk until melted. Whisk in 1½ teaspoons of the vanilla.

Strain the mixture into a bowl or pitcher and divide among 6 cups or dessert bowls. Let pudding cool then top with plastic wrap pressed directly on the surface to prevent a skin from forming. Refrigerate until cold, at least 2 hours.

While the puddings are chilling, make the meringues.

Preheat the oven to 400 degrees. Line a microwave-safe flat tray with a

Serves 6

piece of parchment paper. If you don't possess such a thing, you can use a small cutting board or flip over a Pyrex baking dish.

Beat the reserved egg white with an electric mixer until foamy. Gradually add the remaining 2 tablespoons of granulated sugar and beat until stiff peaks form. Add the remaining ¼ teaspoon vanilla and beat until well blended.

Spoon the mixture into a small plastic storage bag and snip off ½ inch from one of the bottom corners. Pipe the meringue onto the prepared baking tray in twelve 1-inch (give or take) squares. Moisten your finger with a bit of water and gently push down any little peaks. Place the meringues in the microwave and cook on the highest power for 30 seconds. Remove the meringues from the microwave, dust generously with the confectioners' sugar, and transfer with the parchment paper to a baking sheet.

Bake in the preheated oven for 4 minutes, or until lightly golden brown. The meringue should feel crispy on the outside but soft and marshmallowy in the center. Let cool completely. The meringues can be made an hour or two ahead.

To serve, remove the puddings from the refrigerator for a few minutes to take the chill off. Using a spatula, gently slide the meringues off the parchment paper and top each pudding with two meringues.

Arborio Rice Pudding

Using the same rice used to make risotto results in an incredibly rich and creamy rice pudding. The lemon peel adds just the right touch of acidity to balance the richness. This is gluten-free comfort food at its best!

Serves 6

½ cup arborio rice
2 cups whole milk
2 cups half-and-half
¼ cup agave nectar
Pinch of kosher or fine sea salt

Two 1-inch strips of lemon zest
¾ teaspoon pure vanilla extract
Ground or grated cinnamon for
    garnish

Place all the ingredients except the vanilla and cinnamon in a large saucepan and bring just to a boil over medium-high heat. Turn the heat down to medium-low and simmer gently, stirring occasionally, for 30 to 40 minutes, or until the rice is very soft and plump.

Take the pudding off the heat, fish out the lemon strip (it is possible that it will have totally dissolved, if so don't worry), and stir in the vanilla.

Spoon the pudding into six dessert bowls, grate some cinnamon stick on top (or tap some ground cinnamon through a small wire strainer), and serve immediately.

Dairy-Free Chocolate Pots

• Dairy-free
• Grain-free

Serves 6

This simple but elegant dessert has only four ingredients, so use the best quality dark chocolate you can get your hands on. I prefer to use block chocolate that I chop into small pieces, but in a pinch I have used good quality, dairy-free chocolate chips with excellent results.

Make sure the mixture does not get too hot, or you will scramble the egg when whisking it in. If you keep the heat on low and the water at just under a simmer all will be well.

One 13.5-ounce can coconut milk (not light)
9 ounces dairy-free, bittersweet chocolate, chopped (about 1½ cups) or good quality chocolate chips

1 teaspoon pure vanilla extract
1 large egg, lightly beaten
Berries for garnish, optional

Bring 2 inches of water to a simmer in large saucepan. Turn the heat to low and keep the water at a bare simmer.

Shake the can of coconut milk well and pour into a heatproof mixing bowl set over the saucepan of barely simmering water, without the bottom touching the water. Add the chocolate and melt, stirring occasionally. Once the chocolate has melted, whisk in the vanilla and then the egg. Continue whisking over the heat until the mixture is smooth.

Transfer the mixture into a pitcher or spouted measuring cup for easy pouring, and divide among 6 small tea or cappuccino cups or ramekins and chill for 3 hours. The chocolate pots can be made a day ahead.

Garnish with fresh berries when serving, if desired.

Coconut Pudding

In almost as little time as it takes to prepare boxed pudding you can whip up this dairy-free version. The juxtaposition of the subtly flavored creamy pudding with sweet, crunchy coconut flakes is pure bliss to any coconut lover.

• Dairy-free

Serves 4

2 large egg yolks

One 13.5-ounce can coconut milk

1/3 cup granulated sugar

1/4 cup cornstarch

1/4 teaspoon kosher or fine sea salt

1 teaspoon pure vanilla extract

1/2 teaspoon pure almond extract

1/4 cup sweetened flaked coconut

Beat the egg yolks lightly in a medium mixing bowl and set aside.

Shake the can of coconut milk well. Combine the sugar, cornstarch, and salt in a medium saucepan and whisk together. Gradually add the coconut milk and whisk to combine. It is a good idea to run a spatula around the bottom edges to make sure all the cornstarch is incorporated into the coconut milk. Bring to a boil over medium heat and boil for 1 minute, whisking constantly. It is possible that the mixture will start pulling away from the sides of the pan. If this happens stop cooking even if a full minute has not elapsed; the mixture has thickened enough. Pour a little of the hot coconut milk mixture into the beaten egg yolks and whisk well. Gradually whisk in the rest of the coconut milk. Whisk in the extracts. Strain the mixture into a clean bowl and let cool.

Place the coconut flakes in a dry skillet and toast over medium heat until brown and fragrant, 2 to 3 minutes. Once the coconut starts to brown, stir it constantly and don't take your eyes off of it as it burns quickly.

Divide the coconut pudding among 4 dessert bowls. This pudding can be eaten warm or cold. If preparing ahead, press a piece of plastic wrap directly on the surface of the pudding to keep a skin from forming. Refrigerate. Remove from the refrigerator a few minutes before serving to take the chill off.

Top with toasted coconut and serve.

Crème Brûlée

• Grain-free

Once during a whirlwind girlfriends' trip to New York with my dear friends Angie and Randee, we tried to cram in as many restaurant meals as possible. Some days we would eat five or six times and almost invariably ended up ordering crème brûlée for dessert.

On one day we had scheduled back-to-back meals with various friends and at the end of our second meal in as many hours our current dining companion insisted we order crème brûlée over our protests that we couldn't possibly eat another bite. The poor guy never had a chance to lift his spoon before the three of us had devoured it. Apparently we gals do not subscribe to the idea that one can have too much of a good thing.

This restaurant classic is easy to prepare and involves the use of my favorite gadget—the kitchen blowtorch.

3 cups heavy whipping cream	⅓ cup sugar plus ½ cup for topping
6 large egg yolks	1 teaspoon pure vanilla extract

Preheat the oven to 300 degrees.

In a large saucepan, heat the heavy cream until it is very hot but not boiling. Set aside.

Whisk the egg yolks with ⅓ cup of the sugar in a large mixing bowl. Slowly add the hot cream to the egg yolks, whisking constantly. Add the vanilla and mix well. Strain the mixture through a strainer or fine sieve into a pitcher or measuring cup with a spout and handle. Pour the mixture into six 7-ounce ramekins, filling them almost full.

Place the ramekins in a baking pan, put in the oven, and carefully pour very hot water into the pan until it comes halfway up the sides of the ramekins. Bake the custards for 30 to 40 minutes, or until they are set but not dry looking. Remove the ramekins from the water bath and let cool to room tempera-

ture. Refrigerate until cold, at least 1 hour. The custards can be made up to 2 days ahead.

Prior to serving, sprinkle a rounded tablespoon of sugar evenly on the top of each ramekin and heat the sugar with a kitchen blowtorch until the sugar caramelizes evenly. Move the torch slowly and constantly while caramelizing to prevent scorching in spots. Allow the custards to set at room temperature until the sugar hardens, 2 to 3 minutes.

If you do not have a kitchen blowtorch, place the custards under a hot broiler about 3 inches from the heat source and broil until the sugar has caramelized. Watch closely!

Pumpkin Crème Brûlée

- Grain-free
- Dairy-free

Pumpkin pie lovers will flip for this creamy, dairy-free dessert and it makes for a nice alternative to pumpkin pie for your Thanksgiving dinner. The raw turbinado sugar gives the caramelized topping a bit of texture as it does not melt as evenly as granulated sugar. For a more traditional crème brûlée topping, substitute granulated sugar for the raw before torching.

One 13.5-ounce can coconut milk

One 15-ounce can pure pumpkin puree (not pumpkin pie filling)

5 large egg yolks

1/3 cup firmly packed light brown sugar

1 teaspoon pure vanilla extract

1 teaspoon ground cinnamon

1/4 teaspoon ground cloves

1/4 teaspoon freshly grated nutmeg

1/4 teaspoon kosher or fine sea salt

1/2 cup raw turbinado sugar (or granulated sugar)

Preheat the oven to 300 degrees.

Shake the can of coconut milk well. In a large saucepan, heat the coconut milk until it is very hot but not boiling. Set aside.

Whisk the pumpkin, egg yolks, and light brown sugar together in a large mixing bowl. Add the vanilla, cinnamon, cloves, nutmeg, and salt. Whisk well. Slowly add the hot coconut milk while whisking. Strain the mixture through a strainer or fine sieve into a pitcher or measuring cup with a spout and handle. Pour the mixture into 6 ramekins, filling them almost full.

Place the ramekins in a baking pan and carefully pour very hot water into the pan until it comes halfway up the sides of the ramekins. Bake the custards for 30 to 40 minutes, or until set but not dry looking. Remove the ramekins from the water bath and let cool to room temperature. Refrigerate until cold, at least 2 hours. The custards can be made up to 2 days ahead.

Prior to serving, sprinkle a rounded tablespoon of turbinado sugar evenly on the top of each ramekin and heat the sugar with a kitchen blowtorch until

the sugar caramelizes evenly. Move the torch slowly and constantly while caramelizing to prevent scorching in spots. Allow the custards to set at room temperature until the sugar hardens, 2 to 3 minutes.

If you do not have a kitchen blowtorch, place the custards under a hot broiler about 3 inches from the heat source and broil until the sugar has caramelized. Watch closely!

oops... vanilla extract

Zabaglione

• Grain-free

Serves 4

This is a grown-up, romantic dessert, which perfectly illustrates how, in cooking, the combination of a few fairly simple ingredients can be transformed into something very special. The soft, silken texture and spirited taste are the perfect complement to fresh berries. Grand Marnier can be substituted for the Marsala wine, and gives the zabaglione a wonderful orange flavor.

Use the egg whites to whip up a batch of amaretti or macaroons to serve alongside if you wish.

6 large egg yolks	¹⁄₂ cup Marsala wine
¹⁄₃ cup sugar	2 cups chopped berries

Bring about 2 inches of water to a simmer in a large saucepan (or you can use a double boiler).

Place the egg yolks and sugar in a large, heatproof mixing bowl and set the bowl over the saucepan of simmering water. Beat the egg yolks and sugar for about 1 minute. Add the wine and continue to cook and beat until the mixture is light, thick, and tripled in volume, about 5 minutes. The mixture should be the texture of a light pudding or mousse. If you do not beat it long enough it will still be delicious but will tend to separate. Let the mixture cool slightly.

Spoon the berries into four individual serving dishes or wine goblets and top with the zabaglione. Serve immediately.

Plum Clafoutis

Serves 6

A beautiful green, glazed, ceramic baking dish my husband and I bought in the Provence region of France inspired me to come up with gluten-free clafoutis recipes.

Clafoutis is a French dessert that is made by baking fresh fruit in a batter and is traditionally made with unpitted cherries. While I appreciate the sentiment of purists who claim the pits release an intense cherry flavor as they cook, I am uncertain as to how to politely spit out the pits while eating.

Almost any fruit can work in a clafoutis, but I find stone fruits particularly suitable and plum clafoutis are a family favorite.

1 tablespoon unsalted butter plus more for greasing the baking dish

½ cup granulated sugar plus more for dusting the baking dish

1¼ pounds plums, pitted and sliced

1 cup whole milk

¼ cup cornstarch

2 large eggs plus 1 large egg yolk

½ cup heavy whipping cream

Confectioners' sugar for dusting, optional

Preheat the oven to 425 degrees. Butter a round baking dish that is approximately 10 inches in diameter and 1½ inches deep. Add some sugar and swirl it around to coat. Tap out any excess sugar.

Melt the butter over medium-high heat in a large skillet and add the sliced plums. Cook for 5 minutes. Let cool while making the batter.

In a small bowl, whisk together the milk and cornstarch until smooth.

In another bowl, whisk the eggs with the extra egg yolk. Add the sugar and whisk well. Add the cream and whisk until completely blended, then whisk the cream and milk mixtures together. Layer the plums in the prepared dish. Pour the batter over the plums and bake the clafoutis for about 30 minutes or until the batter is set and golden brown.

Dust with confectioners' sugar before serving, if desired.

Chocolate Cherry Clafoutis

• Dairy-free

Serves 6

This is a dairy-free version of clafoutis. I think the subtle coconut flavor from the coconut milk works especially well with the chocolate and cherries.

You can certainly use fresh cherries in this recipe, but the use of canned cherries means you can make this dessert any time of the year.

1½ cups canned coconut milk (shake can well before measuring)

¼ cup cornstarch

¼ cup unsweetened cocoa powder

2 large eggs plus 1 large egg yolk

½ cup granulated sugar plus more for dusting baking dish

Two 14.5-ounce cans tart red cherries in water, drained

Confectioners' sugar for dusting, optional

Preheat the oven to 425 degrees. Spray six 7-inch individual flat ramekins or one large round baking dish approximately 10 inches in diameter and 1½ inches deep with some gluten-free, nonstick cooking spray. Add some sugar and swirl it around to coat. Tap out any excess sugar.

In a medium bowl, whisk together the coconut milk, cornstarch, and cocoa powder until smooth and lump-free.

In another bowl, whisk the eggs with the egg yolk. Add the sugar and whisk well. Mix the coconut milk mixture with the egg mixture.

Layer the drained cherries in the bottom of the baking dish(es) and pour the batter over the cherries. Bake the clafoutis for about 30 minutes, or until the batter is set.

Let cool slightly and dust with confectioners' sugar, if desired. Serve lukewarm.

Kahlúa and Cream Syllabub

꧁꧁꧁꧁꧁꧁꧁꧁꧁꧁꧁꧁꧁꧁꧁꧁꧁꧁

Syllabub is an old-fashioned English dessert traditionally made with cream, sugar, and wine. With the addition of chocolate and Kahlúa I have updated this recipe and transported it to Mexico.

- Grain-free

Serves 6

²/₃ cup semisweet chocolate
   chips

¹/₄ cup freshly brewed strong
   coffee or espresso

3 tablespoons Kahlúa

2 large egg whites

¹/₃ cup sugar

1 cup mascarpone cheese,
   at room temperature

2 cups heavy whipping cream

1 teaspoon pure vanilla
   extract

Chocolate-covered espresso
   beans for garnish, optional

Place the chocolate chips, coffee, and Kahlúa in a small, microwave-safe bowl and microwave for about 1 minute, or until the chocolate is melted and smooth, stirring every 20 seconds. Or melt it in a heatproof bowl set over a pan of gently simmering water, stirring until melted and smooth; the bottom of the bowl should not touch the water.

Using an electric mixer fitted with a whisk attachment, whisk the egg whites on high speed until soft peaks form, then gradually add half of the sugar, whisking until stiff peaks form.

In a large mixing bowl, stir the mascarpone cheese with the melted chocolate mixture until well blended. Gently fold in the egg whites until the mixture is no longer streaky.

In a clean bowl with clean beaters, whip the cream with the remaining sugar and the vanilla until soft peaks form being careful not to overwhip the cream.

Divide the chocolate mixture evenly among six 6-ounce serving dishes or glasses. Top with whipped cream and garnish with chocolate-covered espresso beans. Refrigerate about 2 hours, or until the chocolate is set.

Coconut Mango Panna Cotta

- Dairy-free
- Grain-free

As my formative years were spent in the Philippines, I think I was predisposed to love mangos and silken smooth desserts. This dairy-free panna cotta is a luscious yet light combination of both—perfect for a hot summer's evening.

Typically a panna cotta is unmolded and you should feel free to do so if you prefer, but I think it looks so pretty served in a little dish with a couple mango slices shooting out the top and just a small sprinkle of toasted coconut for crunch and color.

3 medium mangos	One 13.5-ounce can coconut milk
Honey or agave nectar, optional	¼ cup sugar
3 tablespoons water	⅓ cup sweetened flaked coconut
1 envelope unflavored gelatin	for garnish

If you plan to unmold the panna cottas spray six 6-ounce ramekins lightly with gluten-free, nonstick cooking spray. If you are going to serve the panna cotta unmolded, skip spraying the ramekins.

Cut two of the mangos as close to the large seed in the middle as possible, cutting off two cheeks per mango. Remove the skin and cut the flesh into chunks and puree in the blender until very smooth. Taste the puree, and if it is not sweet enough for you, add a small squeeze of honey or agave nectar, being careful not to overpower the flavor of the mango. Push the mango puree through a fine strainer to remove any fibrous strands.

Put the water in a small microwave-safe bowl and sprinkle the gelatin over it. Let set for 5 minutes. Microwave the gelatin for 10 seconds on high power to melt.

Shake the can of coconut milk well. Put the coconut milk and sugar in a small saucepan over medium heat, stirring to dissolve the sugar. Heat just to the boiling point. Whisk the gelatin mixture into the coconut milk well, then whisk in the mango puree. Divide the mixture evenly among the ramekins, cover with plastic wrap, and refrigerate until set, 4 to 5 hours. The panna cottas can be prepared a day ahead.

Preheat the oven to 350 degrees.

Spread a layer of the flaked coconut on a baking pan and bake for 10 to 15 minutes, stirring a few times. Watch the coconut carefully as it can go from toasted to burnt in a matter of seconds. Let cool completely.

Just before serving cut the third mango into 12 slivers for garnish.

If unmolding the panna cotta to serve it, run a sharp knife around the edges of each ramekin and place a small serving plate on top. Flip the plate and ramekin over and the panna cotta should slip out of the ramekin onto the plate. If it does not then take a hot towel and place it on the ramekin for a few seconds. Garnish with the mango slices and toasted coconut.

If you choose not to unmold the panna cotta, then simply stick a couple mango spears into the top and sprinkle on a little toasted coconut.

Mochaccino Mousse

• Grain-free

Serves 6

A favorite coffee shop drink becomes a mousse ideal for an elegant ending to a special meal. I like to prepare these in cappuccino cups for a whimsical presentation and grate some cinnamon on top using a fine Microplane grater but a sprinkling of ground cinnamon works just as well.

Start this recipe a day ahead to allow the mousse to set properly.

1 cup semisweet chocolate chips
½ cup freshly brewed strong
    coffee or espresso
4 large eggs, separated, at room
    temperature

¾ cup heavy whipping
    cream
Freshly grated cinnamon stick
    or ground cinnamon for
    garnish

Place chocolate and coffee in a small, microwave-safe bowl and microwave for about 1 minute, or until the chocolate is melted and smooth, stirring every 20 seconds. Or place the chocolate in a heatproof bowl set over a saucepan of barely simmering water, stirring occasionally until the chocolate is melted and smooth; the bottom of the bowl should not touch the water. Let cool slightly, about 5 minutes, then whisk in the egg yolks.

Using an electric mixer, beat the egg whites on high speed until stiff peaks form. Stir one-fourth of the egg whites into the chocolate mixture and then gently fold in the remaining egg whites.

Spoon the mousse into six 6-ounce cups or glasses and refrigerate overnight to set. Please note that eggs will be uncooked.

Prior to serving, whip the unsweetened cream until soft peaks form. To serve dollop a generous portion of cream onto each mousse and grate a little cinnamon on top or tap a little ground cinnamon on top through a fine, wire strainer.

Dairy-free Pumpkin Pie, page 149

Raspberry White Chocolate Mousse,
page 213

Cocoa Pudding, page 195

Coconut Mango Panna Cotta, page 208

Crème Brûlée, page 200

Dairy-free Chocolate Pots, page 198

Coconut Ice Cream, page 222

Peanut Butter Ice Cream, page 225

Classic Vanilla Ice Cream, page 221

Balsamic Strawberry Ice Cream, page 224

Dairy-free Fudge Pops, page 229

Banana Nut Bread, page 259

Lemon Ricotta Pancakes, page 269

Blueberry Muffins, page 249

Zucchini Muffins, page 257

Stuffed Crepes with Orange Sauce,
page 273

Peanut Butter and Jelly
Ice Cream Sandwiches,
page 232

Rhubarb Fool

• Grain-free

Serves 4

A fool is a classic British dessert made with cooked fruit folded into whipped cream. Much research on my part failed to provide an explanation of the origin of the name. Personally I believe it is because this luscious dessert fools people into thinking you spent a lot of time and effort when in truth nothing could be easier!

For this fool I prefer to layer the cream and rhubarb rather than fold them together. The contrasting layers look so pretty when served in a glass dish.

1 pound fresh rhubarb, cut crosswise into ½ inch slices, or thawed frozen cut rhubarb

2 tablespoons granulated sugar

Freshly squeezed juice of 2 medium oranges (about ¾ cup)

1¼ cups heavy whipping cream

½ cup firmly packed light or dark brown sugar

Put the rhubarb, granulated sugar, and orange juice in a medium saucepan over medium heat. Stir to dissolve the sugar. Bring the mixture to a simmer, cover the saucepan, reduce the heat to low, and cook for about 15 minutes, or until the rhubarb is soft. Remove the pan from the heat and let the mixture cool.

Using an electric mixer, whip the cream until firm peaks appear. Set aside about ½ cup of the whipped cream for serving.

Spoon about 2 tablespoons of the rhubarb mixture into the bottom of four individual glass serving dishes. Sprinkle 1 tablespoon of brown sugar over the rhubarb mixture. Layer the remaining whipped cream over the rhubarb and then top with the remaining rhubarb mixture. Finish with a dollop of whipped cream on each dish and sprinkle the remaining brown sugar over the top.

Serve immediately, or refrigerate until serving time.

Peppermint Patty Creams

ᓀᓀᓀᓀᓀᓀᓀᓀᓀᓀᓀᓀᓀᓀᓀᓀᓀᓀ

• Grain-free

Serves 6

This is an easy dessert perfect for chocolate and mint lovers. It is reminiscent of a favorite candy treat. This can be made a day ahead for a no-stress dinner party finale.

²/₃ cup bittersweet chocolate
  chips

¼ cup freshly brewed strong
  coffee or espresso

2 large egg whites

3 tablespoons granulated sugar

1 cup cream cheese, at room
  temperature

2 cups heavy whipping cream

¼ teaspoon peppermint extract

Green food coloring

Mint leaves for garnish

Place the chocolate and coffee in a small, microwave-safe bowl and microwave for about 1 minute, or until the chocolate is melted and smooth, stirring every 20 seconds. Or melt the chocolate in a heatproof bowl set over a saucepan of barely simmering water, stirring occasionally until melted and smooth; the bottom of the bowl should not touch the water.

Using an electric mixer fitted with the whisk attachment, beat egg whites on high speed until soft peaks form. Gradually add 2 tablespoons of the sugar, whisking until stiff peaks form.

In a large mixing bowl, stir the cream cheese with the melted chocolate mixture until well blended. Gently fold in the egg whites until the mixture is no longer streaky.

In a clean bowl of an electric mixer fitted with the whisk attachment, whip the cream on high speed with 1 tablespoon of sugar and the peppermint extract until soft peaks form, being careful not to overwhip the cream. Stir in 10 to 15 drops of green food coloring until you achieve the desired shade.

Spoon half of the chocolate mixture evenly into six 6-ounce serving dishes or glasses, then top with the mint cream, and finally add the rest of the chocolate mixture. Refrigerate for 4 hours, or until set. Garnish with fresh mint leaves.

Raspberry White Chocolate Mousse

White chocolate mousse is something I normally find too cloyingly sweet but the addition of slightly tart raspberries cuts through the sweetness and marries beautifully with the richness plus it tints the concoction a delicate almost-mauve color.

Of course you can serve the mousse in any dessert dish but for a très elegant presentation, try making these simple chocolate bowls. Your guests will be ever so impressed! Make extra and stash them in the freezer and the next time you need to serve store-bought ice cream for dessert you will have the perfect vehicle on hand to fancy it up. Best part? No need to wash the serving bowls.

MOUSSE

1½ cups fresh raspberries
1 to 3 tablespoons sugar
1½ cups heavy whipping cream
1¼ cups premium white chocolate chips
Grated bittersweet chocolate for garnish, optional

CHOCOLATE BOWLS

6 small balloons (water balloons work perfectly)
6 ounces semisweet chocolate chips

To make the mousse, puree 1 cup raspberries in the blender with 1 tablespoon of sugar. Taste the puree and add more sugar if needed. You want the raspberries sweetened but still slightly tart. Strain through a sieve and discard the seeds. Set aside.

In a medium saucepan over low heat, combine ½ cup of the cream with the white chocolate chips and cook, stirring, until the chips are melted and the mixture is smooth. Remove from heat, stir in the raspberry purée, and let cool to at least lukewarm.

Whip the remaining 1 cup cream until fairly stiff peaks form. Fold the raspberry-white chocolate mixture into the cream in three additions. Refrigerate until the mixture is cold and has firmed up, at least half an hour. The

mousse can be made a few hours ahead, covered with plastic wrap, and kept refrigerated.

Give the mousse a quick whisk and spoon into chocolate bowls (or any dessert bowls). Top with the remaining raspberries and grated chocolate, if using.

Make the chocolate bowls. Holding the tops of the balloons wash them with soap and water so your bowls don't taste like rubber. Let dry completely. Blow up the balloons and tie a knot at the end. Line a baking sheet with wax or parchment paper.

Place the chocolate chips in a microwave-safe bowl and microwave for 1½ to 2 minutes, stirring a couple of times until the chocolate has melted. Scrape the chocolate onto a dinner plate and let cool to lukewarm; if the chocolate is too hot it will pop the balloons and you will have a big mess on your hands.

Holding one balloon at the tied end, place it straight down into the chocolate and slowly lower the side of the balloon into the chocolate about one-third of the way up the side of the balloon. Lift it back up straight, turn the balloon slightly, and repeat; this will create a petal effect at the top edge of the bowl. Continue until the bottom portion of the balloon is thickly coated with chocolate. Hold the balloon straight up and place it on the lined baking sheet, pressing down gently to create a flat bottom. Repeat with remaining balloons. Refrigerate the chocolate-dipped balloons for at least half an hour, or until the chocolate is hard.

To remove the balloon, place your forefinger and thumb under the knot and cut the knot while holding tight. Slowly release the air from the balloons. If you release the air too fast the bowl will break. Remove the balloon. If you have trouble getting the balloon out of the bottom of the bowls, place them in the freezer for a few minutes.

The chocolate bowls can be made several days ahead and stored in the refrigerator. For longer storage place them in the freezer, well covered with plastic wrap or in a freezer-weight, plastic storage bag.

Orange Soufflé with Crème Anglaise

This classic dessert can certainly seem intimidating but by following a few tips you can make this at home easily.

First of all, as oven temperatures vary and since the heat of the oven is a crucial element, do not try this for the first time for the most important dinner party of your life; practice a time or two to get it down first.

Secondly, soufflés absolutely must be served immediately or they deflate. With a little time management you can solve this problem. I make the Crème Anglaise and the egg yolk mixture ahead. Then get someone else to clear the table and prepare the coffee while you whip the egg whites and get them in the oven. It is a good idea to serve these after a heavier meal where the guest will appreciate a few minutes break before dessert.

Thirdly, have serving plates or a tray set up for transporting the soufflés from oven to table as they are too hot to handle comfortably with bare hands.

7 large eggs	3 tablespoons Grand Marnier or
1 cup whole milk	freshly squeezed orange juice
1/2 cup plus 2 1/2 tablespoons	1 teaspoon finely grated orange
granulated sugar	zest
Pinch of kosher or fine sea salt	1 teaspoon cornstarch
1 teaspoon pure vanilla extract	Confectioners' sugar for dusting

Separate the egg yolks from the egg whites. Place the whites in a large mixing bowl, 2 of the yolks in a separate medium mixing bowl, and the remaining 5 yolks in a large heatproof mixing bowl. Lightly beat the 2 egg yolks.

Heat the milk with 2½ tablespoons of the sugar and a pinch of salt in a medium saucepan until it is simmering. Whisk the heated milk into the beaten yolks very gradually. Pour the mixture back into the saucepan and heat over low heat, whisking constantly, for about 3 minutes, or until the mixture is the thickness of heavy cream. If the crème anglaise appears to be curdling, take it off the heat immediately and whisk the daylights out of it or pour it into a blender and give a whirl until smooth. Stir in the vanilla, pour it into a clean bowl through a strainer, and let cool. Pour into a small pitcher for serving. If making the sauce ahead of time, place a piece of plastic wrap directly on the surface to keep a skin from forming, and refrigerate until ready to serve.

Put an inch or two of water in a large saucepan and bring it to a simmer. Turn the heat down to low. Whisk the 5 remaining egg yolks with the remaining ½ cup of sugar until thick and light yellow in color. Place the mixing bowl over the saucepan of barely simmering water and cook until thick and bubbly, about 3 minutes. Take off the heat and whisk in the Grand Marnier or orange juice and the orange zest. Let the mixture cool, whisking occasionally. (I fill my sink with cold water and place the mixing bowl in it to hasten the process.) This can be made ahead as many as several hours. Cover with plastic wrap and refrigerate until ready to beat the egg whites.

Preheat the oven to 400 degrees. Butter six 12-ounce ovenproof ramekins and sprinkle with sugar, tipping and rotating the ramekins to coat the bottom and sides with the sugar. Tap out the excess sugar. (This can be done ahead as well.)

Once the oven is preheated, in an electric mixer fitted with the whisk attachment, beat the egg whites on high speed until soft peaks form. Turn off the mixer, sprinkle on the cornstarch, and turn the mixer back on to high speed. Continue to beat until stiff, slightly dry-looking peaks form.

Whisk the egg yolk mixture quickly and carefully fold into the egg whites, one-third at a time, until blended. Divide the mixture among the prepared ramekins. Smooth the tops and then run your finger around the inside of the rim making a groove in the mixture. Place the ramekins on a baking sheet and immediately into the oven. Bake for 5 minutes, turn the oven temperature down

to 350 degrees, and continue to bake for another 12 minutes, or until the souf-flés are puffed and golden brown on top. Dust with confectioners' sugar and serve immediately. Serve the crème anglaise on the side. To eat, have your guests make a little hole in the top of the soufflé with their spoon and pour a few tablespoons of the sauce into the middle.

Frozen Delights

Classic Vanilla Ice Cream

૮ૈૐૌૐૌૐૌૐૌૐૌૐૌૐૌૐૌૐૌૐૌૐૌૐ

Sometimes the term "vanilla" is used to describe something that is not very excit-ing, dull and unimaginative. Oh, how I beg to differ! Rich, custardy, and flecked with tiny vanilla seeds, this ice cream is a testament as to why vanilla is by far the most favored ice cream flavor.

Makes about 1 pint ice cream

2 cups half-and-half
1 vanilla bean, split in half
    lengthwise
Pinch of kosher or fine sea salt

6 large egg yolks
$1/2$ cup sugar
1 teaspoon pure vanilla extract

Place the half-and-half, vanilla bean, and salt in a medium saucepan and bring to a simmer. Remove from the heat, cover the pan, and let steep for 15 minutes, or longer.

Remove the vanilla bean from the liquid and scrape the seeds back into the pan. Discard the vanilla pod. Reheat until the mixture just comes to a boil.

In the bowl of an electric mixer fitted with the whisk attachment, beat the egg yolks and sugar on medium speed until light and very thick. Turn the speed to low, and very slowly pour the hot half-and-half into the egg yolk mixture. Beat until well combined. Pour the mixture into a clean saucepan and heat over low heat, stirring constantly, until the mixture is thick enough to coat the back of a spoon. Take off the heat and stir in the vanilla. Strain the mixture into a bowl through a fine sieve, let cool, and then refrigerate until cold, about 2 hours.

Pour the chilled custard into an ice cream maker and process for 25 to 30 minutes, or according to the manufacturer's directions. The ice cream will be on the soft side but can be eaten right away, or put into the freezer to "cure" or harden up for a couple hours. Stored in an airtight container, the ice cream will keep at least a week in the freezer.

Coconut Ice Cream

- Grain-free
- Dairy-free

Makes about
1 quart ice
cream

This ice cream is simplicity at its best. Take four ingredients, whirl them in the blender for 30 seconds, and let your ice cream maker take it from there. The best part is that this dairy-free dessert is every bit as rich as its dairy counterpart.

To add a little crunch and contrast to the creaminess, top with some toasted flaked coconut.

Two 13.5-ounce cans coconut
 milk, chilled
²/₃ cup firmly packed light brown
 sugar

Pinch of kosher or fine sea salt
1 teaspoon pure vanilla
 extract
1 cup sweetened flaked coconut

Pour all the ingredients for the ice cream into a blender and whirl them around for about 30 seconds. Pour the mixture into an ice cream maker and process for 25 to 30 minutes, or according to the manufacturer's directions. The ice cream will be on the soft side but can be eaten right away, or put into the freezer to "cure" or harden up for a couple hours.

Preheat the oven to 350 degrees.

Spread a layer of the coconut on a baking sheet and bake for 10 to 15 minutes, stirring a few times. Watch the coconut carefully as it can go from toasted to burnt in a matter of seconds. Let cool, then use as a topping for the ice cream.

Coffee Sorbet

I normally make this recipe with strong decaffeinated coffee so I can enjoy it at night and still get to sleep. The addition of Kahlúa not only enhances the coffee flavor but keeps the sorbet softer and less icy in texture. If you have a concern about the alcohol then by all means leave it out. The sorbet will freeze harder once placed in the freezer and will have a texture closer to a granita.

Try topping this sorbet with some lightly whipped, unsweetened heavy cream—there are simply no words to describe how utterly fantastic it is as the sweet coffee and thick cream melt and combine in your mouth. It is not necessarily a requirement, but I recommend closing your eyes and slowly savoring the moment!

- Grain-free
- Dairy-free

Makes about
1 quart sorbet

³/₄ cup water

³/₄ cup sugar

2 cups very strong coffee
(decaf is fine)

2 tablespoons Kahlúa,
optional

Combine the water and sugar in a small saucepan and bring to a boil over high heat, stirring to dissolve the sugar. Pour the sugar mixture into the coffee, add the Kahlúa, and stir well. Let cool and then refrigerate until cold (or you can put it in the freezer for about half an hour). Pour into ice cream maker and process according to the manufacturer's directions. Place in a covered container and freeze 2 to 3 hours to harden. The sorbet can be made a week ahead.

Balsamic Strawberry Ice Cream

• Grain-free

Makes about
1 quart ice
cream

Strawberries and balsamic vinegar have an affinity for each other as do strawberries and cream. Mix the two and it is a veritable love-fest in the mouth. The vinegar flavor is not too pronounced; it just adds a certain depth to the strawberries. For those with more daring palates, increase the vinegar to as much as double and cook it a bit longer.

2 cups fresh strawberries, hulled
and diced

3 tablespoons balsamic vinegar

¾ cup plus 2 tablespoons sugar

4 cups half-and-half

1 teaspoon pure vanilla extract

Place the strawberries, balsamic vinegar, and the 2 tablespoons of sugar in a medium saucepan and bring to a boil over medium-high heat. Stir to dissolve the sugar. Turn the heat down to low and continue to cook, stirring occasionally, until the vinegar mixture is syrupy, about 5 minutes. Pour into a bowl, let cool, and then put in the refrigerator or freezer until cold.

When strawberries are cold whisk the half-and-half with the remaining ¾ cup sugar and vanilla, then stir in the strawberries. Pour the mixture into an ice cream maker and process for 20 to 30 minutes, or according to the manufacturer's directions. Serve as is, or place in a covered container and freeze until hard, about 6 hours.

Peanut Butter Ice Cream

There is something so fun about this ice cream. Rich, creamy, sweet with just a hint of salt, peanut butter ice cream is a special treat—especially when topped with dark fudge sauce! Use creamy peanut butter for a smooth ice cream or crunchy for a bit of texture.

• Grain-free

Makes about 1 quart ice cream

1 cup peanut butter
½ cup sugar
Pinch of kosher or fine
    sea salt

1½ teaspoons pure vanilla
    extract
2 cups half-and-half
1 cup heavy whipping cream

Using a handheld mixer, cream the peanut butter, sugar, salt, and vanilla in a large bowl until smooth. Add 1 cup of half-and-half and beat on low speed until well mixed. Add the rest of the half-and-half and the cream and whisk by hand—if you try to use your mixer you will end up with it splattering all over the kitchen.

Pour the mixture into ice cream maker and process for 25 to 30 minutes, or according to the manufacturer's directions. The ice cream will be on the soft side but can be eaten right away or put into the freezer to "cure" or harden up for a couple hours. Stored in an airtight container, the ice cream will keep at least a week in the freezer.

Sugar-Free Chocolate Gelato

~~~~~~

• Sugar-free

Makes about
1 quart gelato

Deprivation of any kind is not something of which I am particularly fond. On those few occasions where it becomes necessary to shed a few pounds I find a few bites of something rich, decadent, and chocolaty keeps the cravings in check and makes the whole process much more palatable.

Gelato is made with milk so it is lower in fat and calories than ice cream and since this recipe calls for agave nectar instead of refined sugar, I feel almost virtuous savoring a few bites of this silken frozen treat.

3 cups whole milk
Pinch of kosher or fine sea salt
$^2/_3$ cup agave nectar (light
   or amber)

$^3/_4$ cup unsweetened cocoa
   powder
$1^1/_2$ tablespoons cornstarch

Heat 2 cups of the milk, salt, and agave nectar in a saucepan over medium heat until it comes to a simmer.

In a medium mixing bowl, whisk together the remaining 1 cup of milk, the cocoa powder, and cornstarch until smooth. Add the mixture to the heated milk and agave mixture. Raise the heat and bring to a boil, stirring constantly. Once it starts to boil, continue to cook for 1 minute. Strain the mixture into a clean bowl and let cool to room temperature. Cover with a piece of plastic wrap pressed directly on the surface to keep a skin from forming and refrigerate until cold, about 6 hours. Or to hasten the process, put it in the freezer for 1 hour.

Pour the mixture into an ice cream maker and process for 20 to 30 minutes or according to the manufacturer's directions. Place in a covered container and freeze until hard, about 6 hours.

No-churn Peach Ice Cream

There is a time for fresh peaches and the preparation involved (peeling, pitting, and chopping) and there is a time for a frozen dessert recipe that is almost embarrassingly simple. This recipe is for the latter.

With its jewel-like chunks of semifrozen peaches suspended in the pale, creamy ice cream, this dessert is so beautiful no one need know it was whipped together in mere minutes with a pantry staple of jarred peaches.

One 24-ounce jar (or can) cling peach slices in light syrup, drained	1½ cups heavy whipping cream ¾ cup confectioners' sugar

Line a 9 × 5-loaf pan with two layers of plastic wrap, allowing the plastic wrap to hang over the sides.

Puree 1 cup of the drained peach slices in a blender. Chop the rest of the peach slices into ½-inch chunks.

Whip the cream with the confectioners' sugar until stiff peaks form. Do not overbeat. Gently fold the pureed peaches and peach chunks into the whipped cream. Fill the prepared pan with the mixture, pull the plastic wrap over the top of the ice cream, and freeze for at least 4 hours, or up to 2 days.

To serve, unmold the ice cream, peel off the plastic wrap, and slice. It is best to serve this on chilled plates.

Tropical No-churn Ice Cream

• Dairy-free

Serves 6 to 8

This dairy-free, no-churn ice cream is just the thing to beat the heat. It's creamy and refreshing, requires no ice cream maker, and takes about three minutes of actual work.

The trick to making this work is cold. I refrigerate the Cream of Coconut overnight, put the beaters and mixing bowl in the freezer for a few minutes before making the ice cream, and freeze the whole concoction for at least 8 hours.

This is best served in cold dishes—frozen coconuts optional!

One 15-ounce can Cream of Coconut	$^3/_4$ cup confectioners' sugar
	$^3/_4$ cup mango nectar

Refrigerate the can of Cream of Coconut and mango nectar overnight. Place a large mixing bowl and beaters in the freezer for about 5 minutes before making the ice cream.

Put the cold Cream of Coconut into the cold mixing bowl and add the confectioners' sugar. The Cream of Coconut will be partially solidified at the top and more watery at the bottom; this is normal as the cream rises to the top and gets more solid. Beat on high speed until the Cream of Coconut gets very thick (like lightly whipped cream), add the mango nectar, and mix until well blended. Spoon the ice cream into a plastic or glass container with a snug-fitting lid, smooth it down to compact it, and freeze for at least 8 hours or overnight.

The frozen ice cream will be a soft, not solidly frozen mixture. For best result serve this in cold dishes or coconut halves that have been placed in the freezer for a couple hours.

Dairy-free Fudge Pops

With no dairy or refined sugar in them, you can feel good about handing one of these fudge pops to children. But honestly I just use the kids as an excuse to have these on hand in the freezer for when a chocolate craving strikes me.

- Sugar-free
- Dairy-free

Makes 6 to 8 pops, depending on the size of your molds

One 13.5-ounce can coconut milk

2 teaspoons cornstarch

¾ cup agave nectar (light or amber)

½ cup unsweetened cocoa powder

2 teaspoons pure vanilla extract

Shake the can of coconut milk very well and combine ¼ cup with the cornstarch. Set aside.

In a medium saucepan, whisk the remaining coconut milk, agave, and cocoa powder. Bring to a simmer over medium heat, whisking frequently. Add the cornstarch mixture to the heated coconut milk mixture, raise the heat, and bring to a boil, stirring constantly. Continue to cook for 1 minute once it starts to boil. Remove from heat and stir in the vanilla. Strain the mixture into a clean pitcher or spouted measuring cup and let cool to room temperature.

Pour the cooled mixture into popsicle molds and freeze until firm, about 5 hours.

To release the fudge pops from the molds, it may be necessary to set the molds in hot tap water for a few seconds.

Tangy Lemon Sorbet with Sweet Meringues

• Dairy-free

I love the flavors of lemon and meringue and was trying to figure a way to translate that into a frozen dessert when a famous bad boy chef came to the rescue.

In Gordon Ramsay's stunning cookbook Three Star Chef he breaks down recipes from his famous restaurant and teaches the reader how to prepare the dishes at home. His desserts are complex, architectural masterpieces often comprising several components in one dish. While the complexity of the finished desserts may be intimidating for the average home cook, the techniques described are very doable. I adopted Chef Ramsay's quick-and-easy method of making meringues with a couple very minor adjustments.

LEMON SORBET

1 cup granulated sugar

1 cup water

1 cup freshly squeezed lemon juice

1 tablespoon finely grated lemon
   zest

MERINGUES

2 large egg whites

3 tablespoons granulated sugar

1 teaspoon pure vanilla extract

Confectioners' sugar for
   dusting

Lemon zest for garnish,
   optional

Fresh mint leaves for garnish,
   optional

To make the sorbet, combine the granulated sugar and water in a small saucepan and cook over medium heat until the sugar is completely dissolved. Stir in the lemon juice and zest. Cool to room temperature and then refrigerate until cold, or you can put it in the freezer for about 45 minutes. Pour the mixture into an ice cream maker and process 20 to 30 minutes, or according to manufacturer's directions. Place the sorbet in a covered container and freeze until ready to serve.

Preheat the oven to 400 degrees.

Make the meringues. In the bowl of an electric mixer fitted with the whisk attachment, beat the eggs until foamy starting on low speed and gradually increasing to high. Gradually add the granulated sugar and beat until stiff, glossy peaks form. Turn off the mixer, add the vanilla, and mix well but do not overbeat.

Place a piece of parchment paper on a microwave-safe flat tray. (If you don't possess such a thing you can use a small cutting board or flip over a Pyrex baking dish.) Spoon the egg whites into a plastic food storage bag and snip off ½ inch from one of the bottom corners. Pipe the meringue into 4-inch-long strips. Moisten your finger with a bit of water and gently push down any little peaks. Place the meringues in the microwave and cook on the highest power for 30 seconds. Remove the meringues from the microwave, dust generously with the confectioners' sugar, and transfer the parchment paper with the meringues onto a baking sheet. Unless you have an enormous microwave you will need to do the microwaving in batches and then bake them all at once.

Bake the meringues in the preheated oven for 4 minutes, or until lightly golden brown. The meringue should feel crispy on the outside but soft and marshmallowy in the center. Let cool completely. The meringues can be made 1 to 2 hours ahead.

To serve, using a spatula, carefully transfer the meringues to serving plates allowing two per person. (The underside of the meringue can be sticky, so I dip the spatula in some confectioners' sugar to make this job easier.) Serve the meringues with a scoop of lemon sorbet, and garnish with lemon zest and a sprig of fresh mint, if desired.

Peanut Butter and Jelly Ice Cream Sandwiches

• Grain-free

Makes 8 ice cream sand-wiches

There are no two ways about it, these are just fun! Peanut butter ice cream with jelly sandwiched between peanut butter cookies—pretty much a kid's dream dessert. I'm no kid, but I am a big fan as well. Use any flavor jelly or jam you like, I am particularly fond of strawberry and grape.

Bake the cookies smaller and these make great bite-size treats for birthday parties.

1 recipe Peanut Butter Ice Cream (page 225)
1 recipe Peanut Butter Cookies (page 102)

¾ cup jelly or jam, at room temperature

Prepare the peanut butter ice cream and let harden in the freezer for about 6 hours.

Prepare the dough for the peanut butter cookies and divide the dough into 16 walnut-size balls. Proceed with the recipe from there, baking the cookies 10 to 12 minutes at 350 degrees. Let cool completely.

To assemble the ice cream sandwiches remove the ice cream from the freezer and let it stand at room temperature for about 5 minutes to soften slightly.

Spread a layer of jam on the flat side of each peanut butter cookie. Place a scoop of peanut butter ice cream in the center of half the cookies, on top of the jam. Top with the remaining cookies, jam side down. Gently squeeze the cookies together until the ice cream and jam come to the edges of the cookies. Put the ice cream sandwiches back in the freezer for at least 15 minutes to harden the jam. These can be made 2 days ahead. Place them in a large plastic storage bag or airtight container and store in the freezer.

Raspberry and White Chocolate Terrine

• Grain-free

Admittedly there is a bit of standing over a warm stove holding a mixer involved in making this frozen treat, but it is mindless work that I find oddly refreshing. There is something to be said for staring off into the middle distance, unable to answer the phone or the doorbell, letting your mind wander aimlessly.

This fancy party dessert can be prepared two days ahead so whatever small effort is expended beforehand pays off nicely on party day.

RASPBERRY LAYER

One 12-ounce bag frozen raspberries, thawed

2 tablespoons sugar

1 tablespoon Chambord or other
   berry-flavored liqueur

½ teaspoon freshly squeezed
   lemon juice

WHITE CHOCOLATE LAYERS

3 ounces good-quality white
   chocolate, chopped

¾ cup sugar

¼ cup water

6 large egg yolks

2 teaspoons pure vanilla extract

1²/₃ cups heavy whipping cream

SAUCE

One 12-ounce bag frozen raspberries, thawed

1 tablespoon Chambord or other
   berry-flavored liqueur

Fresh raspberries for garnish,
   optional

Mint leaves for garnish, optional

Line a 9 × 5-inch loaf pan with two layers of plastic wrap, allowing the plastic wrap to hang over the sides.

Prepare the raspberry layer. Put thawed berries, sugar, Chambord, and lemon juice in the blender. Blend until smooth. Strain into a medium mixing bowl and set aside.

Prepare the white chocolate layers. Melt the white chocolate in the microwave for 2 to 3 minutes, stirring occasionally. Or melt the chocolate in a heatproof

bowl set over a saucepan of barely simmering water, stirring occasionally; the bottom of the bowl should not touch the water. Set aside.

Combine the sugar, water, and egg yolks in a medium, heatproof mixing bowl. Place the bowl over a saucepan of barely simmering water. Using a hand-held mixer, beat the mixture continuously for 8 minutes, occasionally scraping down the sides of the bowl with a spatula. The mixture should be thick and pale yellow. Remove the bowl from the saucepan, beat in the melted white chocolate and vanilla, and continue to beat until the mixture is cool.

With clean beaters in a clean bowl, whip the cream on high speed until stiff peaks form. Using a spatula gently mix about one-fourth of the cream into the white chocolate mixture until well blended. Fold the remaining cream into the mixture. Take about 1⅓ cups of the white chocolate mixture and mix it with the strained raspberry mixture.

Fill the prepared loaf pan with about one-third of the white chocolate mixture. Freeze for 30 minutes. Cover the white chocolate layer with the raspberry mixture and cover that layer with the remaining white chocolate mixture. Smooth the top. Pull the plastic wrap over the top of the terrine and freeze for at least 4 hours or up to 2 days.

Prepare the sauce. Place the thawed raspberries and Chambord in a blender and blend until smooth. Strain through a fine mesh strainer to remove the seeds. Can be prepared up to a day ahead. If storing for more than one hour refrigerate in a covered container.

To serve, unmold the terrine, peel off the plastic wrap, and slice. Serve on chilled dessert plates. Drizzle with sauce and garnish with fresh berries and mint leaves, if desired.

Chocolate Cherry Praline Semifreddo

• Grain-free

Semifreddo is an Italian specialty that literally means half-frozen. In this version the chocolate causes the cherry flavor to explode while the praline adds a touch of sweetness and crunch to the lightly almond-flavored cream.

Let the semifreddo stand at room temperature for about 5 minutes before serving and the cherry juice will start to drip slightly, creating a bit of a sauce. Frozen cherries work really well in this recipe if fresh are not in season; no need to defrost them.

PRALINE
½ cup sliced almonds

½ cup granulated sugar

SEMIFREDDO
2 cups fresh or frozen Bing cherries, pitted and halved

One 4-ounce bar bittersweet chocolate, coarsely chopped

4 large egg whites

Small pinch of kosher or fine sea salt

¼ cup sugar

1½ cups heavy whipping cream

1 teaspoon pure vanilla extract

½ teaspoon pure almond extract

Line a 9 × 5-inch loaf pan with two layers of plastic wrap allowing the plastic wrap to hang over the sides. Line a baking sheet with a piece of parchment paper.

Make the praline. Put the almonds in a large skillet over medium heat and toast lightly, about 2 minutes. Add the sugar and cook, stirring occasionally, until the sugar has melted and the almonds are completely coated. Pour the almonds onto the prepared baking sheet, spread them out in an even layer, and let cool. Once the praline is cool and has hardened, break it up into very small pieces with your hands or chop it up with a knife. Place in the freezer for a few minutes to get it cold. The praline can be made several days ahead and stored in a freezer-weight storage bag in the freezer.

Serves 6 to 8

To make the semifreddo, combine the cherries with the chopped chocolate and praline. Put in the freezer while preparing the rest of the ingredients.

In the bowl of an electric mixer fitted with the whisk attachment, beat the eggs and salt until foamy starting on low speed and gradually increasing to high. Gradually add the sugar and beat until stiff, glossy peaks form.

In a clean bowl, beat the cream with the extracts until stiff peaks form. Fold the cream mixture into the egg white mixture. Gently fold the cherry, chocolate, praline mixture in.

Spread the mixture into the prepared loaf pan. Pull the plastic wrap over the top to cover, and freeze until firm, about 6 hours. The semifreddo can be made up to 3 days ahead.

To serve, unmold the semifreddo, peel off the plastic wrap, and slice. Serve on chilled plates.

"Chips and Salsa"

My son Dustin's wedding to the lovely Sarah was the inspiration for this dessert. Like the wedding this is fun, whimsical, and special without being too formal. Great desserts like great marriages take wonderful ingredients and combine them in a way that the resulting combination is so much greater than the sum of the parts.

If you do not have an ice cream maker, or do not feel inclined to make your own ice cream, simply stir two teaspoons or more of ground cinnamon into a quart of softened gluten-free vanilla or coconut ice cream and then pop it back into the freezer to harden back up.

ICE CREAM
Two 13.5-ounce cans coconut milk, chilled

$2/3$ cup firmly packed light brown sugar

2 to 3 teaspoons ground cinnamon

Pinch of kosher or fine sea salt

1 teaspoon pure vanilla extract

CHIPS
4 corn tortillas

1 large egg white

1 tablespoon granulated sugar

1 teaspoon ground cinnamon

SALSA
1 papaya, peeled, seeded, and cut into $1/2$-inch dice

1 pound strawberries, hulled, and cut into $1/2$-inch dice

1 tablespoon chopped fresh mint leaves

Pour all the ingredients for the ice cream into a blender and whirl around for about 30 seconds. Pour the mixture into an ice cream maker and process for 25 to 30 minutes, or according to the manufacturer's directions. The ice cream will be on the soft side but can be eaten right away. Or put it into an airtight container and place in the freezer to "cure" or harden up for a couple hours. The ice cream can be made as much as a week or more ahead.

Makes 8
servings

To make the chips, preheat the oven to 375 degrees. Line a baking sheet with parchment paper or a silicone baking mat.

Cut the corn tortillas in half and cut each half into 3 triangles.

Whisk the egg white in a small bowl until foamy. Brush the chips with the egg white.

Mix the sugar with the cinnamon and sprinkle evenly on the chips. Place the chips on the prepared baking sheet and bake for 10 minutes or until they are crispy and the topping has browned. Let cool. The chips can be made a day ahead and stored in a plastic food storage bag or other airtight container.

To make the salsa, mix the fruit and mint together in a medium bowl. The salsa can be made up to a couple hours ahead. Store in the refrigerator in an airtight container.

To assemble, scoop ice cream into individual serving bowls. Top with the fruit salsa and garnish with the chips. Serve immediately.

Frozen Tiramisu

When I first decided to try my hand at making a frozen version of the famous Italian dessert tiramisu it seemed easy enough; layer mascarpone ice cream with coffee sorbet and there you have it. But one of the essential ingredients in tiramisu is the coffee- and Marsala wine-soaked ladyfingers. While I am sure I could have come up with a gluten-free ladyfinger recipe, it just seemed to lengthen the runway considerably. As a solution I added a Kahlúa meringue layer as a base, which I whipped up in just a few minutes.

Don't be intimidated by the number of steps in this recipe as none are difficult and all can be made in stages and ahead of time. If time does not permit topping the meringue base with the frozen layers just before serving, then assemble the whole thing on a serving platter and stick it back in the freezer; the meringue layer will flatten out a bit but will still taste perfectly delicious.

The chocolate shards turn the dish into a showstopper, but you can get by just fine with a dusting of cocoa powder.

MASCARPONE ICE CREAM LAYER

8 ounces mascarpone cheese, at room temperature
¼ cup granulated sugar
1 cup heavy whipping cream
1 teaspoon pure vanilla extract

COFFEE LAYER

1 recipe Coffee Sorbet (page 223) (the texture will be best if you make it with the Kahlúa)

MERINGUE LAYER

2 large egg whites
2 tablespoons granulated sugar
2 tablespoons Kahlúa
1 tablespoon confectioners' sugar

CHOCOLATE SHARDS

2 ounces bittersweet chocolate chips

Invert a 9 × 5-inch loaf pan on a piece of parchment paper and trace around the top with a pencil. Set aside for the meringue layer. Line the loaf pan with two layers of plastic wrap, allowing the plastic wrap to hang over the sides.

Prepare the mascarpone ice cream layer. In the bowl of an electric mixer fitted with the paddle attachment, cream the mascarpone cheese with the sugar until smooth.

In a clean mixing bowl, beat the cream and vanilla with the whisk attachment on high speed until stiff peaks form. Take a scoop of whipped cream and stir it into the mascarpone cheese mixture to lighten it, then gently fold in the rest of the whipped cream. Spread the mixture evenly in the bottom of the prepared pan and freeze for about 1 hour.

Prepare the coffee sorbet and layer it over the mascarpone cheese layer. You can make the coffee sorbet well ahead, store it in a suitable container, and then scoop it onto the cheese layer. Pull the plastic wrap up to cover, and freeze the layers until really firm, about 5 hours or up to several days.

Preheat the oven to 400 degrees.

Prepare the meringue layer. In the bowl of an electric mixer fitted with the whisk attachment, beat the eggs until foamy, starting on low speed and gradually increasing to high. Gradually add the granulated sugar and beat until stiff, glossy peaks form. Turn off the mixer, add the Kahlúa, then turn the mixer back on, and mix well but do not overbeat.

Take the reserved parchment paper you traced on earlier and place it, pencil side down, on a microwave-safe flat tray. If you don't possess such a thing you can use a small cutting board or flip over a Pyrex baking dish. Mound the beaten egg white mixture on the parchment paper and, using a spatula, spread it out in an even layer extending slightly over the pencil marks.

Microwave on high power for 1½ minutes. If your microwave does not have a turntable or the tray is too large to allow it to turn, then microwave for 45 seconds, turn the tray 90 degrees, and microwave for another 45 seconds.

Remove the meringue from the microwave, put the confectioners' sugar in a small strainer or sieve, and dust the meringue evenly. Transfer the meringue, parchment and all, onto a baking dish and bake in the preheated oven for 5 minutes, or until golden brown. The meringue should feel crispy on the outside but soft and marshmallowy in the center. Remove the meringue, still on the parchment paper, to a wire rack to cool completely.

To make chocolate shards, tear off two pieces of wax paper about 14 inches long. Set aside.

In a microwave-safe bowl, melt the chocolate chips in the microwave for about 2 minutes, stirring every 20 seconds, until the chocolate is almost all melted. Or melt the chocolate in a heatproof bowl, and set over a saucepan with an inch or two of barely simmering water; the bottom of the bowl should not touch the water. Stir the chocolate until fully melted and glossy.

Spread the melted chocolate onto one of the pieces of wax paper in a thin, even layer. Top with the other piece of wax paper and roll it up into a narrow tube, an inch or less in diameter. The narrower the tube, the smaller the shards. Place in the refrigerator, seam side down, for at least 2 hours.

Remove the tube from the refrigerator and quickly unroll it while it is still cold. Remove the top sheet of wax paper and slide a large metal offset spatula under the chocolate. Place the shards on a baking dish and return to the refrigerator until ready to use. When working with chocolate shards, work quickly as your fingers will cause the chocolate to melt.

To assemble the tiramisu place the cooled meringue layer on a chilled serving platter. Unmold the ice cream and sorbet from the loaf pan, remove the plastic wrap, and place on top of the meringue, coffee side down. Top with chocolate shards or dust with some cocoa powder tapped through a small strainer or sieve. Serve immediately or place back in the freezer until ready to serve. Cut into slices and serve on chilled dessert plates.

Dark Fudge Sauce

Makes about 2 cups sauce

It is said that the right accessory completes the outfit. This dark fudge sauce is like the perfect pair of diamond earrings; rich, luxurious, and classic. Poured over ice cream it hardens just enough, molding to the cold contours but maintaining its fudgy character.

If you are concerned about the fat content or want a dairy-free version, substitute water for the heavy cream and leave out the butter. The sauce will not be as thick but, if anything, the deep chocolate flavor will be intensified and it will still be a hundred times better than anything you can buy in a jar.

3/4 cup heavy whipping cream
Small pinch of kosher or fine sea
   salt
1/2 cup sugar
1/2 cup corn syrup or agave
   nectar

1/2 cup dark, unsweetened cocoa
   powder, measured then sifted
2 tablespoons unsalted butter
1 teaspoon instant espresso
   powder
1 teaspoon pure vanilla extract

Combine the cream, salt, sugar, corn syrup or agave nectar, and cocoa powder in a medium saucepan. Bring to a gentle boil over medium heat. Reduce the heat to low and simmer for 5 minutes, stirring frequently. Remove from heat and stir in the butter, espresso powder, and vanilla. Let cool. The sauce will thicken as it cools. Stir again before serving.

Use the sauce warm, or pour it into a glass jar and refrigerate for later use. To warm, remove the lid and reheat the sauce in the microwave. Or take the lid off the jar and place the jar in a pan of simmering water until warm.

The sauce will keep, covered, in the refrigerator for up to 1 week.

Salted Caramel Sauce

When I was young we had an old-fashioned ice cream maker—the kind you pack with rock salt and ice and crank by hand! My sisters and I would swear we would do the churning but would quickly bail, leaving my dad to do all the work.

My favorite part of the ice cream was that bit right at the top where some of the salty water seeped into the cold cream. This salted caramel sauce gives ice cream that subtle saline bite even though now I have an electric ice cream maker.

Use a good sea salt or in a pinch (pardon the pun) kosher salt but please, please, please do not use table salt; it is far too harsh and bitter.

- Grain-free

Makes about
1½ cups sauce

---

1 cup sugar

4 tablespoons (½ stick) unsalted butter, cut into 4 pieces

½ cup heavy whipping cream

1½ to 2 teaspoons good sea salt (depending on your taste)

Make sure all your ingredients are measured and ready to go before starting this sauce. Heat the sugar over medium-high heat in a large, deep, heavy-bottomed saucepan. (Use a pan that is much larger than you think you will need as the cream splatters and the sugar gets very hot.) Once the sugar starts to liquefy, whisk it vigorously and continue whisking until it comes to a boil. Once it comes to a boil, stop whisking. If you need to, you can gently swirl the pan to ensure even browning of the sugar. Continue to boil the sugar until it turns a deep amber color; like an old penny.

Take the pan off the heat and quickly stir in the butter. Add the cream slowly while whisking. The mixture will expand considerably and bubble and spurt so be very careful. Stir in the sea salt. Let the mixture cool in the pan for 5 to 10 minutes, then pour into a glass jar with a lid. Let cool completely and store, covered, in the refrigerator for up to two weeks.

To warm, remove the lid and reheat the sauce in the microwave. Or take the lid off the jar and place the jar in a pan of simmering water until warm.

Morning Treats

Apple-Cinnamon Muffins

Surprisingly buttery in flavor considering the total absence of any dairy, these grain-free muffins not only taste great but also make your house smell amazing while they are baking.

What a way to wake up!

- Grain-free
- Dairy-free
- Sugar-free

Makes 12 muffins

3 cups blanched almond flour
1 teaspoon baking powder
1/2 teaspoon baking soda
1 1/2 teaspoons ground cinnamon
1/2 teaspoon kosher or fine
    sea salt

2 large eggs
1/2 cup agave nectar
2 teaspoons pure vanilla extract
1 heaping cup unsweetened
    applesauce

Preheat the oven to 350 degrees. Line 12 standard-size muffin cups with paper liners.

In a mixing bowl, whisk together the almond flour, baking powder, baking soda, ground cinnamon, and salt.

In a medium mixing bowl, whisk together the eggs, agave nectar, vanilla, and applesauce. Stir the applesauce mixture into the almond flour mixture and blend well. Divide the batter evenly among the prepared muffin cups.

Bake the muffins for 25 to 35 minutes, or until a toothpick inserted in the center of a muffin comes out clean. Let cool in pan for 15 minutes.

Banana Nut Muffins

Makes 18 muffins

These are my son Colin's favorite muffins and admittedly I have been known to hold them back as bribes to get him to do the dishes. Ingredients for banana nut muffins—a few dollars. A clean kitchen—priceless!

To make this recipe dairy-free, substitute grapeseed (or another flavorless oil) for the melted butter and use coconut or other dairy-free milk.

1½ cups sweet rice flour blend
1 cup sugar
1 teaspoon baking powder
½ teaspoon baking soda
½ teaspoon kosher or
    sea salt
3 ripe bananas

8 tablespoons (1 stick) unsalted
    butter, melted and cooled
    slightly
½ cup whole milk
1 large egg
1 teaspoon pure vanilla extract
1 cup chopped walnuts

Preheat the oven to 350 degrees. Line 18 standard-size muffin cups with paper liners.

In a medium mixing bowl, whisk together the sweet rice flour blend, sugar, baking powder, baking soda, and salt.

In a large mixing bowl, mash 2 of the bananas well with a fork. Add the melted butter, milk, egg, and vanilla and whisk well. Add the banana mixture to the flour mixture and stir until all the flour is blended into the batter. Dice the remaining banana and fold it into the batter along with the chopped walnuts. Divide the batter evenly among the prepared muffin cups, filling them about three-quarters full.

Bake the muffins for 30 to 35 minutes, or until golden brown and a toothpick inserted into the middle comes out clean. Let cool for 5 minutes.

Blueberry Muffins

It would be immodest for me to say these are the best blueberry muffins in the world so let me say this: with their sugary, crunchy tops, moist, cake-like batter bursting with blueberries, and just a hint of lemon, I challenge you to find a better muffin, gluten-free or not.

Frozen blueberries, can be used; thaw slightly before tossing with flour and adding to the batter.

2 teaspoons freshly squeezed lemon juice

1/2 cup whole milk, at room temperature

Zest of 1 lemon, finely grated

1 cup plus 1 tablespoon sugar

2 cups sweet rice flour blend

2 teaspoons baking powder

1/2 teaspoon kosher or fine sea salt

1 pint fresh blueberries

8 tablespoons (1 stick) unsalted butter, at room temperature

2 large eggs, at room temperature

1 teaspoon pure vanilla extract

Preheat the oven to 350 degrees. Spray 12 standard-size muffin cups with gluten-free, nonstick cooking spray and line the muffin cups with paper liners.

Stir the lemon juice into the milk and let set for about 5 minutes. The milk may look a little curdled but this is okay.

In a small bowl, mix the lemon zest with the 1 tablespoon of sugar until fully blended. It is easiest to do this with your fingers as the lemon zest may be moist and tends to clump. Set aside.

In a medium mixing bowl, whisk together the sweet rice flour blend, baking powder, and salt. Put a scant 1/4 cup of the flour mixture in a small bowl, add the blueberries, and toss to coat. Set aside.

In the bowl of an electric mixer fitted with the paddle attachment, cream the butter and the remaining 1 cup sugar together on medium speed until light and fluffy, about 3 minutes. Turn the speed to low, and add the eggs, one at a

Makes 12 muffins

time, mixing until each egg is fully incorporated, scraping down the sides of the bowl with a spatula after each addition. Add the vanilla and mix well. With the mixer on low speed, add the flour mixture and lemon-milk mixture to the creamed butter starting with one-third of the flour mixture, then half the lemon-milk mixture, half the remaining flour mixture, the rest of the lemon-milk mixture, and the rest of the flour mixture. Mix until just combined. Remove the bowl from mixer and scrape down the sides and bottom of the bowl well with a large spatula. Gently fold in the blueberries with any flour left in the bowl into the batter. Divide the batter evenly among the prepared muffin cups, filling the cups almost to the top. Top the batter with the lemon zest-sugar mixture.

Bake the muffins for 30 to 35 minutes, or until the tops are golden brown and a toothpick inserted in the center comes out clean. Let cool for 5 minutes in the pan. Serve warm.

Good Morning Oatmeal Muffins

Like a healthy bowl of oatmeal, these muffins are a great way to start your morning. I like my muffins, like my oatmeal, filled with dried apricots and cherries, but this recipe can be changed up to suit your family's tastes. Add a bit more cinnamon and chopped apples, diced bananas, chocolate chips, raisins, nuts, or any combination you like.

These muffins are also very low in fat. To lower the fat content even more, use two egg whites instead of the whole egg. The low-fat content of the batter causes the muffins to stick to regular paper muffin liners; if it bothers you, bake these in silicone baking cups or in a well-greased nonstick muffin pan.

If you don't have buttermilk, simply stir 1 tablespoon of white vinegar or lemon juice into the milk of your choice (including any dairy-free variety) and let stand for 5 minutes.

1 cup low-fat buttermilk

1 cup certified gluten-free oats

1 cup sweet rice flour blend

1 teaspoon baking powder

½ teaspoon baking soda

½ teaspoon kosher or sea salt

½ cup firmly packed brown sugar

¾ cup unsweetened applesauce

1 large egg

1 teaspoon pure vanilla extract

⅔ cup dried apricots, chopped

⅔ cup dried sweet cherries, chopped

Preheat the oven to 350 degrees. Line 16 standard-size muffin cups with paper liners or silicone baking cups, or grease the cups well with oil or gluten-free, nonstick cooking spray.

In a medium mixing bowl, pour the buttermilk over the oats and let sit for at least 5 minutes, or up to 1 hour; the longer they sit the moister the muffin.

In another mixing bowl, whisk together the sweet rice flour blend, baking powder, baking soda, salt, and brown sugar.

Makes 16
muffins

Add the applesauce, egg, and vanilla to the oats and buttermilk and mix well. Add to the flour mixture and mix until well combined.

Mix together the chopped apricots and cherries. Take a large handful and set aside for the tops of the muffins. Stir the rest of the chopped fruit into the batter. Pour the batter into the prepared muffin cups and sprinkle the reserved chopped fruit on top.

Bake the muffins for 20 to 30 minutes, or until a toothpick inserted into the center comes out clean. Let cool 5 minutes in the pan. Serve warm. The muffins can be made ahead and reheated in the microwave for a few seconds before eating, if desired.

Lemon Streusel Muffins

These muffins have a tang from the lemon and yogurt with a crunchy, sweet streusel topping. I typically use nonfat Greek yogurt, which adds richness without any additional fat, but any kind of yogurt will do. To really bump up the lemon flavor, lemon yogurt is a great substitution.

For a dairy-free version, simply substitute the yogurt with 1 cup coconut milk and use good-quality, butter-flavored substitute instead of the butter.

1 cup nonfat Greek or whole-milk yogurt, at room temperature

2 large eggs, at room temperature

1 teaspoon pure vanilla extract

Juice of 2 lemons

Zest of 2 lemons, finely grated

2½ cups sweet rice flour blend

1 cup plus 1 tablespoon sugar

1 tablespoon baking powder

½ teaspoon kosher or fine sea salt

8 tablespoons (1 stick) cold, unsalted butter, cut into small pieces

1 tablespoon melted butter

Preheat the oven to 350 degrees. Line 12 large-size muffin cups (or 14 to 16 standard-size muffin cups) with paper liners.

In a medium mixing bowl, whisk together the yogurt, eggs, vanilla, lemon juice, and the zest of 1 lemon.

In large mixing bowl, whisk together the sweet rice flour blend, the 1 cup sugar, baking powder, and salt. Cut the cold butter into the flour mixture using a pastry cutter or two knives, or just rub the butter into the flour with your fingertips until the mixture looks like a coarse meal. Take ½ cup of the mixture and set aside in a small bowl for the streusel topping. Stir the yogurt mixture into the flour mixture and blend just until all the flour is incorporated; the batter will be thick. Divide the mixture among the prepared muffin cups.

Add the zest of 1 lemon and the remaining 1 tablespoon of sugar to the reserved flour mixture. Top with the melted butter and stir until the mixture

Makes 12 large muffins or 14 to 16 standard muffins

is clumpy. Sprinkle the reserved streusel topping on top of each muffin. Bake the muffins for 20 to 25 minutes, or until a toothpick inserted into the center comes out clean and the topping is starting to brown. If the muffins are baked but the topping has not yet started to brown, simply turn on the broiler and place the muffins under it for a few seconds being careful not to burn the topping. Let the muffins cool in the pans for 5 minutes, then remove to a wire rack to finish cooling. Serve warm or at room temperature.

Pumpkin Cranberry Muffins

Reminiscent of pumpkin pie, these muffins are the perfect way to start a brisk fall morning. Not only are they moist, fragrant, and nutritious but they also freeze well, making them handy for those rush mornings when you need something you can grab and go.

- Grain-free
- Dairy-free
- Sugar-free

Makes 12 muffins

3 cups blanched almond flour
1 teaspoon baking powder
½ teaspoon baking soda
1½ teaspoons ground cinnamon
¼ teaspoon ground cloves
¼ teaspoon freshly grated nutmeg

½ teaspoon kosher or fine sea salt
2 large eggs
2 tablespoons grapeseed oil
½ cup agave nectar
One 15-ounce can pure pumpkin puree (not pumpkin pie filling)
1½ cups dried cranberries

Preheat the oven to 350 degrees. Line 12 standard-size muffin cups with paper liners.

In a mixing bowl, whisk together the almond flour, baking powder, baking soda, ground cinnamon, cloves, nutmeg, and salt.

In a medium mixing bowl, whisk together the eggs, oil, agave nectar, and pumpkin. Stir the pumpkin mixture into the almond flour mixture and blend well. Fold in the dried cranberries. Divide the batter evenly among the prepared muffin cups.

Bake the muffins for 25 to 35 minutes, or until a toothpick inserted in the center of a muffin comes out clean. Let cool in pan for 15 minutes.

Strawberry-Banana Muffins

◊◊◊◊◊◊◊◊◊◊◊◊◊◊◊◊◊◊◊◊◊◊◊◊◊◊◊◊◊◊◊◊◊

• Sugar-free

Makes 12
muffins

There is no need for butter or jam with these muffins as the strawberry and bananas get all soft and gooey inside. The only accompaniment needed is perhaps a cup of coffee or a glass of milk. I often sprinkle just a touch of granulated sugar on top before baking, which gives a caramelized effect to the strawberry but without this the muffins have no refined sugar.

As a tip, measure the oil first and then the honey with the same measuring spoon. This will help the honey slide off easily.

2 cups sweet rice flour blend
2 teaspoons baking powder
½ teaspoon kosher or fine sea salt
2 ripe bananas, roughly mashed
    (still chunky)
1 cup fresh strawberries, hulled
    and diced
¾ cup whole milk

1 large egg
3 tablespoons grapeseed oil
    (or other neutral-tasting
    vegetable oil)
3 tablespoons honey
1 teaspoon pure vanilla
    extract
6 whole strawberries

Preheat the oven to 350 degrees. Line 12 standard-size muffin cups with paper liners. In a large mixing bowl, whisk together the sweet rice flour blend, baking powder, and salt. Add the mashed bananas and diced strawberries and toss to coat.

In a small mixing bowl, whisk together the milk, egg, oil, honey, and vanilla. Add to the flour mixture and stir until all the flour is combined. Spoon the batter into the prepared muffin cups.

Remove the leaves from the whole strawberries, cut them in half lengthwise, and slice them a few times almost to the top, but leaving the top intact. Fan the berries out slightly and top each muffin. Or you can just place the unsliced strawberry halves on top if that all seems like too much work. Bake the muffins for 30 to 40 minutes, or until the tops are lightly browned. Let cool in the pan for 5 minutes and serve warm.

Zucchini Muffins

I knew I had a hit on my hands when my husband, decidedly not a zucchini lover, devoured three of these in one sitting.

Since frosting a muffin makes it appear dangerously close to a cupcake, we'll just call the luscious cream cheese and sour cream concoction on these zucchini muffins a "topping." The muffins themselves are perfectly terrific on their own; the topping just puts them over the top! If you prefer, serve the topping on the side like a spread, and let each diner decide to top or not.

To make this recipe dairy-free, substitute grapeseed (or other flavorless oil) for the melted butter and forgo the topping.

MUFFINS

2 cups sweet rice flour blend

1 cup granulated sugar

1½ teaspoons baking powder

½ teaspoon baking soda

½ teaspoon kosher or fine sea salt

1 teaspoon ground cinnamon

¼ teaspoon grated nutmeg

2 medium zucchini, grated on the large holes on a box grater (about 2 cups)

8 tablespoons (1 stick) unsalted butter, melted and cooled slightly

2 large eggs, lightly beaten

1 teaspoon pure vanilla extract

¾ cup walnuts, chopped

TOPPING

4 ounces cream cheese, at room temperature

¼ cup sour cream, at room temperature

¼ cup confectioners' sugar

½ teaspoon pure vanilla extract

Chopped walnuts for garnish, optional

Preheat the oven to 350 degrees. Line 12 standard-size muffin cups with paper liners.

In a medium mixing bowl, whisk together the sweet rice flour blend, sugar, baking powder, baking soda, salt, cinnamon, and nutmeg.

Makes 12
muffins

In a large mixing bowl, combine the grated zucchini, melted and cooled butter, eggs, and vanilla. Add this mixture to the flour mixture and stir until the batter is just blended. Stir in the chopped nuts. Divide the batter among the prepared muffin cups.

Bake the muffins for 30 to 35 minutes, or until the tops are golden brown and a toothpick inserted in the center comes out clean. Let the muffins cool in the pan for 5 minutes, then transfer to a wire rack to finish cooling. While the muffins are baking and cooling, make the topping.

Place all ingredients for the topping in a medium mixing bowl and beat until smooth, starting on low speed and gradually increasing to medium-high. Top the cooled muffins with the topping or serve on the side. Refrigerate the topping if not using immediately. If topping the muffins, garnish with chopped walnuts, if desired.

Banana Nut Bread

A great way to use up those bananas that have gone too ripe, this recipe is so simple and requires no heavy machinery—just a spoon and a bowl!

I invariably buy one or two more bananas than we can eat before they get too ripe. So as not to waste them, I put them in the freezer, skin and all, and there they rest for when the urge for banana bread strikes me. The skins on the bananas will get black in the freezer but not to worry. Let them thaw out for about an hour before mashing them up.

Personally I think walnuts are the perfect complement to bananas in this recipe, but feel free to use any nut you prefer.

3 very ripe bananas, mashed with a fork

8 tablespoons (1 stick) unsalted butter, melted and cooled

¾ cup sugar

1 large egg, well beaten

1 teaspoon pure vanilla extract

1 teaspoon kosher or fine sea salt

1 teaspoon baking powder

1½ cups sweet rice flour blend

½ cup nuts, chopped

Preheat the oven to 350 degrees. Lightly spray a 9 × 5-inch loaf pan with gluten-free, nonstick cooking spray.

In a large mixing bowl, mix the mashed bananas with the melted butter. Add the sugar, egg, and vanilla and mix well. Add the salt, baking powder, and sweet rice flour blend, *in that order*, and mix well. Stir in the nuts. Pour the batter into the prepared pan. Bake the banana bread for 50 to 60 minutes, or until a toothpick inserted in the center comes out clean. Let cool in the pan for 15 minutes, then remove from the pan and transfer to a wire rack to cool completely or serve warm.

Orange Cranberry Bread

• Dairy-free

In our house, Santa always leaves oranges in our Christmas stockings. This quick bread makes good use of both the oranges and seasonal cranberries. These also make terrific gifts to take to someone else's home—I divide the batter between 3 small disposable baking pans and bake for about 10 minutes less.

Tossing the cranberries and orange zest with some of the flour mixture before stirring them into the batter helps keep them suspended throughout the bread as it bakes.

BREAD

2 cups sweet rice flour blend

1 cup granulated sugar

1½ teaspoons baking powder

½ teaspoon baking soda

1 teaspoon kosher or fine sea salt

1½ cups fresh or frozen cranberries, chopped

2 tablespoons finely grated orange zest

¾ cup freshly squeezed orange juice (approximately 3 average-size oranges)

2 tablespoons grapeseed oil (or other neutral-tasting vegetable oil)

1 large egg, well beaten

GLAZE

1 cup confectioners' sugar, sifted

1 packed teaspoon finely grated orange jest

1 to 2 tablespoons freshly squeezed orange juice

Preheat the oven to 350 degrees. Lightly spray a 9 × 5-inch loaf pan with gluten-free, nonstick cooking spray.

In a large mixing bowl, whisk together the sweet rice flour blend, granulated sugar, baking powder, baking soda, and salt. Take about ½ cup of the mixture and put in a small mixing bowl, add the chopped cranberries and orange zest, and toss well to coat. Set aside.

Stir the orange juice, oil, and egg into the flour mixture and mix until well blended. Add the cranberries and orange zest along with all the flour mixture they were tossed in and stir well. Pour the batter into prepared pan. Rap the pan three times on the counter to settle the batter.

Bake the bread for 50 to 60 minutes, or until a toothpick inserted into the center comes out clean. Let cool in the pan for 15 minutes, then remove the bread from the pan and transfer it to a wire rack to cool.

Make the glaze. Combine the confectioners' sugar and orange zest with 1 tablespoon of the orange juice in a small mixing bowl and whisk together. You want a thick but pourable consistency; add more orange juice as needed. With the bread still on the wire rack, set over a baking sheet, pour the glaze over the top of the bread letting it drizzle down the sides.

Makes one
9 × 5-inch loaf

Zucchini Nut Bread

• Dairy-free

Makes one
9 × 5-inch loaf

Anyone who has a garden or knows someone who has a garden finds themselves with an abundance of zucchini in the late summer. This moist and delicious bread makes good use of that abundance.

¾ cup walnuts	2 large eggs
1½ cups plus 1 teaspoon sweet rice flour blend	1 cup sugar
1 teaspoon ground cinnamon	½ cup grapeseed oil (or other neutral tasting oil)
½ teaspoon baking powder	1½ cups grated zucchini (1 average-size zucchini)
½ teaspoon baking soda	
½ teaspoon kosher or fine sea salt	1 teaspoon pure vanilla extract

Preheat the oven to 350 degrees. Generously spray a 9 × 5-inch loaf pan with gluten-free nonstick cooking spray.

Chop the walnuts coarsely. Reserve ½ cup of the chopped walnuts and finely chop the remaining ¼ cup. Reserve for later.

In a large mixing bowl whisk together 1½ cups sweet rice flour blend, cinnamon, baking powder, baking soda, and salt. In another large mixing bowl beat the eggs well with a whisk, then add the sugar, oil, zucchini, and vanilla, and whisk until well combined. Add the dry ingredients to the wet ingredients and mix well. Toss the ½ cup of coarsely chopped walnuts with 1 teaspoon sweet rice flour blend and gently mix them into the batter. Pour the batter into the prepared loaf pan. Evenly sprinkle the ¼ cup finely chopped walnuts over the top of the zucchini nut bread.

Bake for 45 to 55 minutes or until a toothpick inserted in the center comes out clean and the top is golden brown. Let cool in the pan for 5 minutes. Run a knife around the edges of the pan and transfer the bread to a wire rack to finish cooling completely.

Peaches and Cream Scones

Unlike cake baking where you want all the ingredients at room temperature, scone baking requires cold ingredients to get the proper texture. If you store your sweet rice flour at room temperature then you can pop the dry ingredients into the freezer for a few minutes, time permitting. I rarely have the patience to do this and my scones come out just fine. I do use cold butter and cream, however.

You can change the flavor of these scones by substituting equal amounts of any dried fruit you like for the dried peaches; apricots and strawberries are particularly lovely. Serve these warm with some butter or, better yet, clotted cream. If you can't find clotted cream then simply shake some heavy cream in a jar to thicken it up a bit and pour the cream over the scones for a heavenly experience.

2 cups sweet rice flour blend

1½ teaspoons baking powder

½ teaspoon kosher or fine sea salt

¼ cup sugar plus more for
    sprinkling

8 tablespoons (1 stick) cold,
    unsalted butter, cut into small
    pieces

¾ cup dried peaches, chopped

1 large egg, lightly beaten

½ cup heavy whipping cream
    plus more for brushing on top

2 teaspoons pure vanilla extract

Preheat the oven to 425 degrees. Line a baking sheet with parchment paper or a silicone baking mat.

In a large mixing bowl, whisk together the sweet rice flour blend, baking powder, salt, and the ¼ cup of sugar. With your fingertips rub the cold butter into the flour mixture until it resembles a coarse meal with some larger pieces of butter still visible. Mix in the chopped dried peaches; I do this with my hands as the dried fruit tends to be sticky when chopped and clumps together; you want the pieces evenly distributed throughout the flour mixture.

Makes 12 to 14 scones

In a small mixing bowl, whisk together the egg, cream, and vanilla. Pour the wet ingredients into the flour mixture and blend until the mixture just starts to come together. Do not overmix or the dough will become too sticky.

Flour a work surface with some sweet rice flour blend, and dump the dough onto the flour. Knead the dough 2 or 3 times to bring it together. Gently pat the dough into a rough circle about ½ inch thick. Cut out the scones using a small cookie cutter or an inverted glass. After you have cut out the circles, push the dough scraps together one more time to get a couple more scones out of it. Place the scones on the prepared baking sheet, brush with a little heavy cream, and sprinkle some sugar on top of each. Bake the scones for about 15 minutes, or until golden brown.

Pumpkin Maple Scones

Pumpkin pie flavorings, rich maple glaze, and toasted pumpkin seeds make for one delicious scone with a variety of textures. Even my husband, not a pumpkin fan, loves these.

The food processor makes quick work of the dough but you can just as easily make these by hand. Simply combine all the dry ingredients, rub the butter in with your fingers, combine wet ingredients, and mix the wet ingredients into the dry.

SCONES

1/2 cup pumpkin seeds

2 cups sweet rice flour blend

1/3 cup firmly packed brown
   sugar

1 1/2 teaspoons baking powder

1/2 teaspoon kosher or fine sea
   salt

1 teaspoon ground cinnamon

1/4 teaspoon grated nutmeg

1/4 teaspoon ground ginger

1/4 teaspoon ground cloves

8 tablespoons (1 stick) cold
   unsalted butter, cut into small
   pieces

1/2 cup canned pure pumpkin
   puree (not pumpkin pie filling)

1/3 cup heavy whipping cream

1 teaspoon pure vanilla extract

GLAZE

1 cup confectioners' sugar

6 tablespoons maple syrup

Preheat the oven to 425 degrees. Line a baking sheet with parchment paper or a silicone baking mat.

Lay the pumpkin seeds on a separate, unlined baking sheet in a single layer and toast the seeds for about 5 minutes, or until they are brown and fragrant. Set aside.

In the bowl of a food processor, combine the sweet rice flour blend, brown sugar, baking powder, salt, cinnamon, nutmeg, ginger, and cloves and pulse several times to combine. Add the butter and pulse quickly 8 to 10 times, or until the flour resembles a coarse meal with some larger pieces of butter remaining.

Makes 8 large scones

Add the pumpkin, cream, and vanilla and pulse a few times just to combine. Do not overprocess or the dough will be too sticky.

Flour a work surface with some sweet rice flour blend and dump the dough onto it. Knead the dough 2 or 3 times just to bring it together. Gently pat the dough into a circle about 9 inches in diameter and ½ inch thick. Cut the dough circle into 8 triangular pieces (like a pie) and place them on the prepared baking sheet.

Bake the scones for 15 minutes, or until they are browned and feel firm to the touch. Let cool slightly on a wire rack set over a baking sheet while making the glaze.

Whisk the confectioners' sugar and maple syrup together until smooth and no lumps remain.

Spoon the glaze over the scones, letting some of it drizzle down the sides, and top with the toasted pumpkin seeds.

Chocolate Cherry Scones

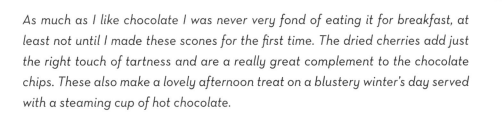

As much as I like chocolate I was never very fond of eating it for breakfast, at least not until I made these scones for the first time. The dried cherries add just the right touch of tartness and are a really great complement to the chocolate chips. These also make a lovely afternoon treat on a blustery winter's day served with a steaming cup of hot chocolate.

2 cups plus 1 tablespoon sweet rice flour blend

1½ teaspoons baking powder

½ teaspoon kosher or fine sea salt

¼ cup plus 2 teaspoons sugar

8 tablespoons (1 stick) cold, unsalted butter, cut into small pieces

½ cup chocolate chips

½ cup dried cherries, chopped

1 large egg, lightly beaten

½ cup heavy whipping cream plus more for brushing on top

1 teaspoon pure vanilla extract

½ teaspoon unsweetened cocoa powder

Preheat the oven to 425 degrees. Line a baking sheet with parchment paper or a silicone baking mat.

In a large mixing bowl, whisk together the 2 cups of sweet rice flour blend, baking powder, salt, and sugar. With your fingertips rub the cold butter into the flour mixture until it resembles a coarse meal with some larger pieces of butter still visible. Mix the chocolate chips and dried cherries with the remaining 1 tablespoon of sweet rice flour, toss to coat, and stir into the sweet rice flour mixture.

In a small mixing bowl, whisk together the egg, cream, and vanilla. Pour the wet ingredients into the dry mixture and blend just until the dough starts to come together. Do not overmix or the dough will become too sticky.

Flour a work surface with some sweet rice flour blend and dump the dough on the flour. Knead the dough 2 or 3 times to bring it together. Gently pat the

Makes 8 large
scones

dough into a rough circle about 8 inches in diameter and ½ inch thick. Cut the dough circle into 8 triangular pieces (like a pie) and place them on the prepared baking sheet. Brush the tops of the scones with some heavy cream. Mix the cocoa powder with 2 teaspoons of sugar and sprinkle on the top of the scones.

Bake the scones for 15 minutes, or until golden brown. Let cool slightly. Serve warm.

Lemon Ricotta Pancakes

These lovely soufflé-like pancakes are a wonderful way to start the day off. As an added benefit, they are low in carbohydrates as well as being gluten-free. Indulgence has never been so healthy!

The pancakes deflate slightly if they sit for very long but are still delicious. Serve with syrup or fresh berries if desired.

- Sugar-free
- Grain-free

Makes about 12 pancakes

4 eggs, separated
8 ounces ricotta cheese, at room
   temperature

Zest of 1 lemon, finely grated
Big pinch of kosher or sea salt

Beat the egg whites on high speed until stiff peaks form.

In a separate bowl, beat the ricotta cheese on medium-high speed until smooth and creamy, about 2 minutes. Add the egg yolks, lemon zest, and salt and beat until very smooth and fluffy. Take a scoop of the egg whites and mix into the yolk mixture to lighten it up, then fold the yolk mixture into the whites.

Heat a griddle or skillet over medium heat until hot, then spray with gluten-free, nonstick cooking spray.

Scoop about one-third cup of the mixture onto the griddle for each pancake. The batter will be really fluffy so push it down slightly with the bottom of the measuring cup to flatten it out a bit. Cook over medium heat until the pancakes are browned on the bottom and cooked through, about 5 minutes. Flip the pancakes over and cook until they feel firm to the touch, another minute or two.

Dutch Baby Pancake

Serves 2

Have the table set and your breakfast companion seated before bringing this heavenly pancake to the table. Crisp, ethereally light, and oh so delicate in flavor, the Dutch baby pancake is a snap to whip up and your oven does most of the work.

You can of course top with maple syrup or fruit, but the traditional way to eat this is with a squeeze of lemon and a dusting of confectioners' sugar; a tradition I happily follow.

2 large eggs
½ cup sweet rice flour blend
½ cup whole milk
Pinch of kosher or fine sea salt

4 tablespoons (½ stick) unsalted
   butter
Fresh lemon wedges
Confectioners' sugar

Place a 10-inch, cast-iron skillet in the oven and preheat to 450 degrees.

With a handheld mixer, whip the eggs, sweet rice flour blend, milk, and salt together all at once, starting on low until the ingredients are combined and then increasing the speed to high for 30 seconds.

Carefully take the hot skillet out of the oven and add the butter to it. Let the butter melt, and then pour the batter into the pan. Return the skillet to the oven and bake the pancake for 12 to 15 minutes, or until puffed and golden brown.

To serve, cut the pancake in half, squeeze a bit of lemon juice on top, and dust generously with confectioners' sugar. Serve immediately.

Egg Crepes

- Grain-free
- Sugar-free

This recipe is a basic that you will use over and over again. The crepes can be folded in triangles and served with a drizzle of warm maple syrup, spread with jam and rolled up, or stuffed with fruit or ricotta cheese—the varieties are endless. And how fabulous is it to eat something that seems decadent but is actually packed with protein and good for you?

Cooking crepes may seem a tad difficult at first but I assure you with a little practice you can whip up a batch in just a few minutes. Use a small nonstick skillet with sloped (not straight) sides or a crepe pan, and heat the pan before pouring in the crepe batter. You want the pan hot enough that a drop of water sizzles up immediately when dropped on it. It is also important to very lightly grease the pan; I spray a light coating of gluten-free, nonstick cooking spray in the hot pan and then wipe it gently with a paper towel so there is just enough grease to keep it from sticking but not enough to keep the crepe batter from spreading evenly around the bottom of the pan. You may need to repeat this process before each crepe. You can have two pans going at the same time, just stagger the process so that one is cooking while you are flipping the other. I find it easiest to use a large silicone spatula for flipping; it is flexible enough to get under the crepe and won't scratch the pan.

Making the batter with cream will give the crepes less of an "eggy" flavor, but this recipe works equally well with milk (including any kind of dairy-free milk) or even water.

The first crepe cooked can be like a first child, a little more difficult than the rest but no worries, if it doesn't turn out properly just put some butter or syrup on it and eat it in the kitchen when no one is looking (the crepe—not the kid).

3 large eggs
3 tablespoons heavy whipping cream, whole milk, or water
Small pinch of kosher or fine sea salt
1 teaspoon pure vanilla extract

Makes about eight 5-inch crepes

Whisk all the ingredients together with either a handheld electric mixer or a whisk. Make sure to whisk until it is thoroughly blended and none of the egg whites are visible.

Heat a small skillet or crepe pan over medium heat until a drop of water sizzles immediately when dropped on the pan. Lightly grease the pan, and pour in 1 tablespoon of batter, tilting and rotating the pan to spread the batter evenly over the bottom of the pan. Cook until the edges look dry and are starting to brown, about 1 minute. Flip over the crepe and cook for 30 seconds on the other side. Remove the crepe to a plate and repeat with the remaining batter.

The cooked crepes can be kept warm in a low (200-degree) oven or reheated briefly in the microwave. The crepes also keep well in the refrigerator for a day, so if you need to make a lot of them, you can make them ahead and reheat before serving.

Stuffed Crepes with Orange Sauce

Here is an example of how mastering a basic recipe, in this case egg crepes, can springboard into all sorts of possibilities.

This is a beautiful breakfast fit for a special day; it seems so fancy but is really very little work. Of course you needn't tell a soul how easy this is; let others think you worked very hard and hopefully someone will offer to do the dishes out of sheer gratitude.

- Grain-free
- Sugar-free

Makes about eight 5-inch crepes

1 recipe Egg Crepes (page 271)

8 ounces cream cheese, at room temperature

1 tablespoon orange zest, finely grated

1 cup freshly squeezed orange juice

1 to 2 tablespoons honey

1 tablespoon cold butter

Prepare the egg crepes and keep warm.

With an electric mixer on medium-high speed, beat the cream cheese with two-thirds of the orange zest (about 2 teaspoons) and 2 tablespoons of the orange juice until the mixture is smooth and creamy. Set aside.

In a small saucepan over medium-high heat, bring the remaining orange juice, zest, and 1 tablespoon of the honey to a boil. Reduce the heat until the mixture is at a low boil and continue to cook until the mixture is reduced to about half a cup and has thickened, about 6 minutes. Whisk in the cold butter until it is melted. Taste the sauce and add more honey, if desired.

Spread the cream cheese mixture on the crepes, spreading it to the edge of each crepe, and fold the crepe into triangles. Serve, topped with the orange sauce.

Peanut Butter Crepes

• Grain-free

Makes about 8
crepes

What kid doesn't like peanut butter? These crepes are packed with protein, but your kids won't care about that. They will care that they taste great and are fun to eat. The obvious filling? Well jelly, of course, and if you fill them with all-fruit preserves, these make a healthy breakfast sure to be gobbled up. I'll let you in on a secret—adults love these just as much as the kids!

The crepes can be kept warm in a low oven or microwaved quickly to reheat just before spreading with jam or jelly and serving.

2 large eggs
3 tablespoons creamy peanut
   butter

3 tablespoons water

With a handheld electric mixer or in a blender, combine all the ingredients and mix until smooth; you will have a thin batter.

Heat a small skillet or crepe pan over medium heat until a drop of water sizzles immediately when dropped on the pan. Spray the pan very lightly with gluten-free, nonstick cooking spray; I spray the pan then wipe it with a paper towel. Ladle 1 tablespoon of the batter onto the hot skillet and immediately tilt and rotate the pan to spread the batter evenly over the bottom. Cook the crepe until the edges look dry and the bottom is browned, about 1 minute. Flip the crepe over and cook the other side for 30 seconds. Keep warm while cooking the rest of the crepes.

Chestnut Crepes

Available in specialty and health food stores, chestnut flour has been used in Italy for centuries. A nut as opposed to a grain flour, it is remarkably low in fat and has a mellow, naturally sweet flavor, making it a welcome addition to a gluten-free diet.

The chestnut crepes alone are fabulous and make for a healthy breakfast treat. I like to roll them with a slight drizzle of melted butter on top. For an over-the-top breakfast treat I stuff them with ricotta chestnut cream and sprinkle with a light dusting of confectioners' sugar.

- Grain-free
- Sugar-free
  (if the
  confectioners'
  sugar is
  omitted)

CHESTNUT CREPES
1 cup chestnut flour
3 large eggs
1¼ cups water

RICOTTA CHESTNUT CREAM
1 cup chestnut flour
¾ cup water
¼ cup heavy whipping cream
1 tablespoon honey
½ cup ricotta cheese
Confectioners' sugar for dusting,
  optional

To make the crepe batter, whisk together the chestnut flour, eggs, and water until smooth. Let stand for 15 minutes. (If making the ricotta chestnut cream, prepare this while the batter is resting.)

Heat a small skillet or crepe pan over medium heat until a drop of water sizzles immediately when dropped on the pan. Lightly grease the pan with oil or a quick spurt of gluten-free, nonstick cooking spray. Add 2 tablespoons of batter to the pan, tilting and rotating the pan to spread the batter evenly over the bottom of the pan. Cook until the edges are curling up and browned, about 1 minute. Flip the crepe over and cook for 30 seconds on the other side. Remove the crepe to a plate. Continue making crepes until the batter is used up, stacking the crepes on top of each other to keep them warm.

To prepare the ricotta chestnut cream, put the chestnut flour, water, cream,

Makes about ten 5-inch crepes

and honey in a blender and blend until smooth, scraping down the sides to ensure everything is well combined. Pour into a small bowl and refrigerate for at least 15 minutes. The chestnut cream can be made a day ahead and stored, covered, in the refrigerator. Stir the ricotta cheese into the chestnut cream and mix well.

When you have finished making the crepes, spread some ricotta chestnut cream on each crepe, fold into triangles, and serve with a light dusting of confectioners' sugar, if desired.

Oatmeal Breakfast Bars

Makes 12 bars

Think of these breakfast bars as oatmeal to go. They just get better as the days go by, so whip up a batch on a lazy Sunday and they will be ready and waiting for you on those hectic weekday mornings.

2½ cups certified gluten-free oats

1 cup sliced almonds

1 cup roasted sunflower seeds

1 cup dried apricots, chopped

1 cup dried cranberries

½ teaspoon kosher or fine sea salt

One 14-ounce can sweetened condensed milk

Preheat the oven to 250 degrees. Heavily spray a 12×9-inch baking dish with gluten-free, nonstick cooking spray.

In a large mixing bowl, combine the oats, almonds, sunflower seeds, chopped apricots, cranberries, and salt. Pour in the condensed milk and mix well with a large spatula. Spread the mixture into the prepared dish and press down firmly and evenly with the spatula.

Bake the bars for 1 hour.

Let cool for 15 minutes, then run a sharp knife around the edges of the pan, and cut into twelve 3-inch squares. Let cool completely.

Store the bars in an airtight container or plastic food storage bag.

Cinnamon Rolls

Not often does my gluten-free life leave me feeling deprived, but I must admit that when I walk by one of those cinnamon roll places in the mall or the airport I have a twinge of envy for people who can tolerate gluten.

Determined to no longer feel deprived, I set out on a quest to make the perfect cinnamon roll. I wanted the buns to be flaky. I did not want to have to use yeast and let them rise (who wants to wait that long!). Most of all I needed them to be delicious. Two weeks and ten pounds later I came up with the perfect recipe.

Gluten-free dough is a double-edged sword; the lack of gluten keeps the rolls from getting tough but also makes the dough harder to work. The method here is equally important as the recipe ingredients.

DOUGH

2 cups sweet rice flour blend, plus more for kneading

1 teaspoon xanthan gum

1 1/2 teaspoons baking powder

1/2 teaspoon baking soda

1/2 teaspoon kosher or fine sea salt

3/4 cup whole milk cottage cheese

1/3 cup buttermilk

1/4 cup granulated sugar

4 tablespoons (1/2 stick) unsalted butter, melted

1 teaspoon pure vanilla extract

FILLING

2/3 cup firmly packed light brown sugar

2 teaspoons ground cinnamon

1/4 teaspoon kosher or fine sea salt

3 tablespoons unsalted butter, melted

1 cup pecans, finely chopped

GLAZE

2/3 cup confectioners' sugar

1 teaspoon pure vanilla extract

2 to 3 tablespoons cold, whole milk

Preheat the oven to 400 degrees. Spray a 9- or 10-inch springform pan lightly with gluten-free, nonstick cooking spray. Lightly spray two 20-inch-long

pieces of parchment or wax paper (parchment is better as it is usually wider) with gluten-free, nonstick cooking spray.

In a large mixing bowl, whisk together the sweet rice flour blend, xanthan gum, baking powder, baking soda, and salt.

In a food processor, combine the cottage cheese, buttermilk, sugar, melted butter, and vanilla. Process until smooth, about 15 seconds. Add the flour mixture and pulse in short bursts until the dough starts to come together. Do not overprocess. This dough will be very soft. Dump the dough onto a work surface lightly dusted with some sweet rice flour blend and knead it with floured hands, 5 or 6 times, until it is smooth. Flatten and shape the dough into a rectangle.

Lay out one piece of the sprayed parchment paper, sprayed side up, on a work surface. Place the dough in the center and top with the other piece of sprayed parchment, sprayed side touching the dough. With a rolling pin, roll the dough into a 12 × 15-inch rectangle.

Make the filling. In a medium mixing bowl, combine the brown sugar, cinnamon, and salt.

Remove the top sheet of parchment paper from the dough, and brush the dough with about 2½ tablespoons of melted butter, reserving some to brush on the tops of the rolls just before baking.

Sprinkle the brown sugar mixture evenly over the dough. Top with the chopped pecans and gently pat them into the dough.

Using the bottom sheet of parchment paper to help you, roll the long side of the dough up jelly-roll style. Pinch the seam together but leave the ends open.

Wrap the dough cylinder up in the parchment and put in the freezer for 20 minutes. You can skip this step if you don't have room in the freezer or are in a hurry, but you get much neater slices by doing this as it firms up the roll.

Unwrap the parchment from the dough and, using a thin, sharp knife, cut the roll into 12 equal pieces, approximately 1¼ inches thick. Set the pieces cut side up on the prepared pan. They should touch each other but don't be

Serves 10 to 12

concerned if there are gaps. Brush the tops of the rolls with the remaining melted butter.

Bake the rolls for 20 to 25 minutes, or until they are firm and golden brown. Let cool in the pan for 5 minutes. While the rolls are baking and cooling make the glaze.

In a small bowl, mix the confectioners' sugar with the vanilla and 2 tablespoons of the milk until smooth. You should have a thick but pourable consistency. If not, add a little more milk.

When the rolls are cool, run a knife around the edge of the pan and remove the outer ring of the springform pan. Run a large knife or offset spatula gently between the rolls and the bottom of the pan. Transfer the rolls to a serving plate. Drizzle the glaze over the tops of the cinnamon rolls and serve.

Doughnuts

Basically sweetened pâte à choux, or cream puff dough, that is fried, this is a simple doughnut (beignet) recipe that can be whipped up quickly and will be gobbled up just as fast!

Heating the oil to the proper temperature will ensure your doughnuts are crispy on the outside, almost creamy on the inside, and not greasy. If you do not have a deep-frying or candy thermometer, test the oil by dropping a bit of the dough into it; if the dough starts to sizzle and cook immediately but doesn't burn, you're good to go.

You can also make these with the dairy-free version of pâte à choux and fry them up in the same manner.

As with any pâte à choux dough, have all your ingredients measured and standing by before starting the recipe.

4 large eggs

8 tablespoons (1 stick) unsalted butter

1 cup water

3 tablespoons granulated sugar

Pinch of kosher or sea salt

1 cup sweet rice flour blend

Confectioners' sugar or cinnamon sugar for dusting

Crack the eggs into a liquid measuring cup or pitcher.

In a medium saucepan, combine the butter, water, sugar, and salt and bring just to a boil over medium heat giving the pan a swirl, or stirring occasionally, to help the butter melt. As soon as the water comes to a boil, turn the heat down to low, and dump in the sweet rice flour blend all at once. Stir quickly and in one direction with a wooden spoon. The liquid will start absorbing the flour and will form into a ball. Continue cooking and stirring for 1 or 2 minutes to cook off some of the liquid. The pan will start to coat with a film of butter.

Dump the dough into the bowl of a standing mixer fitted with the paddle attachment (or use a food processor; see below) and beat the dough for about 1 minute on medium speed to cool it down slightly. Add the eggs, one at a time, mixing until each egg is fully incorporated before adding the next. Continue mixing until the dough is thick and shiny, about 3 minutes.

If you are using a food processor, dump the dough into the machine, process for 30 seconds, and then start adding the eggs, one at a time, through the feed tube. Let the machine whirl for a few seconds to fully incorporate each egg before adding the next. Once all the eggs have been added, let the machine go for about 30 more seconds. Use at once or store, refrigerated, for up to 2 days.

To fry the doughnuts, line a plate with paper towels. Preheat the oven to 200 degrees. Heat about 3 inches of vegetable oil in a heavy saucepan to 375 degrees or use a deep fryer.

When the oil is at the correct temperature, drop tablespoonfuls of dough (I use a small ice cream scoop) into the hot oil and fry for about 5 minutes, or until puffed and golden brown. I gently stir the doughnuts a few times while they are frying to get them evenly browned. Do not fry too many at one time, or it will cool the oil down too much, and you will have greasy doughnuts. I do about 4 or 5 at a time in a large saucepan.

With a slotted spoon or skimmer, remove the cooked doughnuts from the oil and transfer them to paper towels to drain. Place the drained, fried doughnuts in the preheated oven and keep warm while frying the remaining doughnuts.

Dust the doughnuts with confectioners' or cinnamon sugar. Serve warm.

Index